T0334197

Cambridge Elements ≡

Elements in Shakespeare and Text
edited by
Claire M. L. Bourne
The Pennsylvania State University
Rory Loughnane
University of Kent

THEATRE HISTORY, ATTRIBUTION STUDIES, AND THE QUESTION OF EVIDENCE

Holger Schott Syme
University of Toronto

CAMBRIDGE
UNIVERSITY PRESS

CAMBRIDGE
UNIVERSITY PRESS

Shaftesbury Road, Cambridge CB2 8EA, United Kingdom

One Liberty Plaza, 20th Floor, New York, NY 10006, USA

477 Williamstown Road, Port Melbourne, VIC 3207, Australia

314–321, 3rd Floor, Plot 3, Splendor Forum, Jasola District Centre,
New Delhi – 110025, India

103 Penang Road, #05–06/07, Visioncrest Commercial, Singapore 238467

Cambridge University Press is part of Cambridge University Press & Assessment,
a department of the University of Cambridge.

We share the University's mission to contribute to society through the pursuit of
education, learning and research at the highest international levels of excellence.

www.cambridge.org
Information on this title: www.cambridge.org/9781009227414

DOI: 10.1017/9781009227391

First published 2023

A catalogue record for this publication is available from the British Library.

ISBN 978-1-009-22741-4 Paperback
ISSN 2754-4257 (online)
ISSN 2754-4249 (print)

Theatre History, Attribution Studies, and the Question of Evidence

Elements in Shakespeare and Text

DOI: 10.1017/9781009227391
First published online: March 2023

Holger Schott Syme
University of Toronto

Author for correspondence: Holger Schott Syme, holger.syme@utoronto.ca

ABSTRACT: Over the past decade, attribution scholars have come to a consensus that Shakespeare wrote some of the additions printed in the 1602 quarto of Kyd's *Spanish Tragedy*. This new development in textual studies has far-reaching consequences for established theatre-historical narratives. Accounting for Shakespeare's involvement in *The Spanish Tragedy* requires us to rethink the history of two major theatre companies, the Admiral's and the Chamberlain's Men, and to reread much of the documentary record of late Elizabethan theatre. Modelling what a theatre-historical response to new attributionist arguments might look like, the author offers an in-depth reinterpretation of Philip Henslowe's records of new plays, develops a novel account of how theatre companies copied and adapted plays in one another's repertories (including a reconsideration of the "Ur-Hamlet" and the two *Shrew* plays), and reconstructs an early modern cluster of Hieronimo plays that also allows us to reimagine Ben Jonson's career as an actor.

KEYWORDS: Shakespeare, attribution, adaptation, repertory, *Spanish Tragedy*

ISBNs: 9781009227414 (PB), 9781009227391 (OC)
ISSNs: 2754-4257 (online), 2754-4249 (print)

Contents

Introduction: Attribution Studies and Theatre-Historical Evidence

"If the play is a book, it's not play," Stephen Orgel quipped a quarter century ago.[1] Yet the study of playbooks and the study of early modern performance – early modern textual studies and theatre history – have near-identical roots and share a set of foundational figures. Edmond Malone, for instance, was central to the development of editorial practice and equally significant as a theatre historian. Malone was the first to transcribe and publish, in excerpts, the document that continues to shape much of what we think we know about the theatre "of Shakespeare's time," as the phrase goes: the 242 folio leaves bound in limp velum known as Philip Henslowe's "Diary."[2] A century later, W. W. Greg was not only one of the pioneers of the New Bibliography but also the first modern editor of Henslowe's "Diary" (he remains its most in-depth annotator) and the author of the first major study of playhouse manuscripts.[3] The reaction against the New Bibliography was grounded in a richer under-standing of how texts were produced and handled in the theatre, developed by scholars such as Orgel, Tiffany Stern, and Paul Werstine.[4] For as long as plays of the early modern period have been edited for publication, that textual activity has been informed by assumptions about how theatre companies of the period operated. When it comes to dramatic literature, key concepts of twentieth-century bibliography derive as much from theories about the theatrical life of

---

[1] Stephen Orgel, "What Is an Editor?" *Shakespeare Studies* 24 (1996): 23–29, 23.

[2] In *The plays and poems of William Shakspeare, in ten volumes: collated verbatim with the most authentick copies ... to which are added, ... an historical account of the English stage; and notes; by Edmond Malone* (London: Printed by H. Baldwin for J. Rivington and sons [etc.], 1790), 10 vols., vol. 1, part 2, 288–329.

[3] *Henslowe's Diary*, ed. W. W. Greg (A. H. Bullen, 1904–8), 2 vols. (subsequently cited as "Greg"); *Dramatic Documents from the Elizabethan Playhouses* (Clarendon, 1931), 2 vols.

[4] See, for example, Stephen Orgel, *The Authentic Shakespeare and Other Problems of the Early Modern Stage* (Routledge, 2002); Tiffany Stern, *Documents of Performance in Early Modern England* (Cambridge University Press, 2009); Paul Werstine, *Early Modern Playhouse Manuscripts and the Editing of Shakespeare* (Cambridge University Press, 2013).

texts as from Elizabethan and Jacobean printing practices. Often, textual scholars draw on the work of theatre historians to explain puzzling textual features; sometimes, they hypothesize about playhouse practices to arrive at explanations unavailable in the extant theatre historical scholarship. In turn, theatre historians regularly rely on the work editors have done on theatrical documents, from Greg to R. A. Foakes and R. T. Rickert (the most recent editors of Henslowe's manuscript) to the scholars editing Malone Society volumes and the small army of archival gatherers, excerpters, and recontextualizers that produces the *Records of Early English Drama*.

Even though textual studies and theatre historiography have long been interdependent modes of research, often pursued by the same scholars wearing multiple hats, they can appear curiously disconnected. Consider, for instance, the question of revision. That early modern plays, especially Shakespeare's, were frequently revised has become almost a truism in early modern literary studies and editorial theory. Modern theatre historians have been rather more sceptical, with Roslyn Knutson providing strong evidence that revision was not a common practice. Recently, Richard Dutton has expanded that case, arguing that the primary cause for revision was court performance, whereas alterations for regular commercial stagings were a rarity.[5] In this instance, textual scholars have developed a view of broader professional practices from the study of a small corpus of plays produced by a single playwright for a company in which he was also a sharer, largely ignoring the evidence adduced by theatre historians that shows how unrepresentative Shakespeare's situation was. At the same time, theatre history has been slow to respond to the groundswell of research in attribution studies that has dominated textual studies over the past decade. Even as scholarly consensus has emerged about the presence of other playwrights' contributions in a range of Shakespeare texts, and as sophisticated methods of stylometric and statistical analysis have begun to complicate earlier narratives about collaboration, theatre historians have not seriously reexamined established accounts of the relationships between playwrights and companies.

---

[5] Roslyn Knutson, "Influence of the Repertory System on the Revival and Revision of *The Spanish Tragedy* and Dr. Faustus," *English Literary Renaissance* 18 (1988): 257–74; Richard Dutton, *Shakespeare, Court Dramatist* (Oxford University Press, 2016) (subsequently cited as "Dutton").

Attribution scholars have produced ever more specific solutions to the puzzle they set out to address ("who wrote this play?"), but their answers have led to new questions that attribution studies cannot answer. Since these questions concern central issues in early modern theatre history, taking them seriously will require a fundamental rethinking of long-held beliefs.

In this study, I try to model what such a theatre-historical response might look like regarding the now-established view among attribution scholars that Shakespeare wrote at least some of the additional scenes published in the fourth quarto of *The Spanish Tragedy* (1602). This seemingly minor shift in textual thinking has the potential to trigger a full-scale reinterpretation not only of Henslowe's recording practices, but of how early modern repertories were structured. At a more local level, the reattribution necessitates a rereading of the large corpus of allusions to Kyd's play and its performance(s) – a rereading that supports new narratives about *The Spanish Tragedy* as a play in the Chamberlain's Men's (rather than the Admiral's Men's) repertory, a key text in a cluster of dramatizations of the Hieronimo material, and the occasion of a rich intertextual and intertheatrical exchange that continued into the later seventeenth century.

That Shakespeare wrote the 1602 additions is not a wholly new idea. First floated by Coleridge, it was seriously proposed in 1968 in an essay by Warren Stevenson but not reexamined with any rigour until the early 2000s.[6] Then, over the span of just five years, several attribution scholars, using different methodologies from stylistic to statistical analysis, all came to the same conclusion: at least some of the five additional passages published in the 1602 quarto of the play were likely written by Shakespeare.[7] Since then, further

---

[6] Warren Stevenson, "Shakespeare's Hand in *The Spanish Tragedy* 1602," *Studies in English Literature 1500–1900* 8 (1968): 307–21.

[7] Warren Stevenson, *Shakespeare's Additions to Thomas Kyd's* The Spanish Tragedy: *A Fresh Look at the Evidence regarding the 1602 Additions* (Edwin Mellen, 2008); Hugh Craig, "The 1602 Additions to *The Spanish Tragedy*," in *Shakespeare, Computers, and the Mystery of Authorship*, ed. Hugh Craig and Arthur Kinney (Cambridge University Press, 2009), 162–80; Brian Vickers, "Identifying Shakespeare's Additions to *The Spanish Tragedy* (1602): A New(er) Approach," *Shakespeare* 8 (2012): 13–43; Douglas Bruster, "Shakespearean Spellings and

studies, drawing on yet other methodologies and different data sets, have bolstered the case for Shakespeare's authorship, although one of those contributions complicated the narrative.[8] In Gary Taylor's view, the evidence points to Thomas Heywood as the author of the first addition, but he agrees that the longest new passage, "the Painter's part," is probably by Shakespeare.[9] There now exists a remarkable level of agreement, even among scholars who are otherwise sharply divided, that Shakespeare had a major hand in the revisions. An attribution solution on which Gary Taylor and Brian Vickers concur, despite their many acrimonious exchanges in the *TLS* letters pages, must surely be considered as close to settled as such questions can ever be.[10]

For textual scholars, the debate may end there. For theatre historians, though, the attributionists' new answers beg more questions than they resolve: if we now must think of *The Spanish Tragedy* as a play with which Shakespeare was involved in the late 1590s, what does that do to established narratives about company repertories, about casting, and about playwrights' company affiliations? Attribution studies either ignore such questions as outside their purview, provide answers that rely on the very theatre-historical narratives that their findings call into question, or offer explanations that rest on unsupportable assumptions about theatre companies' working practices. It is time to confront these questions head on.

Handwriting in the Additional Passages Printed in the 1602 *Spanish Tragedy*," *Notes and Queries* 60 (2013): 420–4; and José Manuel Rodríguez Herrera, "Much Ado about Whose Fingerprints? Shakespeare's Hand in the 1602 Additions to *The Spanish Tragedy*," *Neophilologus* 99 (2015): 505–20.

[8] Hugh Craig, "Shakespeare and Three Sets of Additions," in *The New Oxford Shakespeare: Authorship Companion*, ed. Gary Taylor and Gabriel Egan (Oxford University Press, 2017), 241–5; David L. Gants, "Mine of Debt: William White and the Printing of the 1602 *Spanish Tragedy* … *with New Additions*," ibid., 231–40; John V. Nance, "Shakespeare and the Painter's Part," ibid., 261–77.

[9] Gary Taylor, "Did Shakespeare Write the *Spanish Tragedy* Additions?" ibid., 246–60.

[10] The *Authorship Companion* also offers a critique of Vickers's methods (Gabriel Egan, "The Limitations of Vickers's Trigram Tests," 60–6) to which Vickers responds in "Shakespeare and the 1602 Additions to *The Spanish Tragedy*: A Method Vindicated," *Shakespeare* 13 (2017): 101–6.

The Spanish Tragedy *and Company Ownership*

The traditional story about *The Spanish Tragedy* has essentially gone unchallenged for more than a century. It goes something like this: Kyd's play, first performed sometime in the late 1580s by an unidentified company, appears in Philip Henslowe's financial records as a mainstay of Lord Strange's Men's repertory in 1592, under the title "Jeronymo" (or "Joronymo"). It is performed sixteen times between March 1592 and January 1593, taking in more than £29, an average of almost £1 17s. per show; only *Henry VI* was more profitable. Subsequently, the play disappears for almost four years and does not feature in the repertory of the Admiral's Men, the next long-term occupants of Henslowe's Rose playhouse, from May 1594 to the beginning of 1597. When a play by the same title reemerges in January of that year, Henslowe, strangely, marks it "ne" – his usual signal that a play was either new or, as Knutson has proposed, "marketably new."[11] It runs for thirteen performances at the Rose before the records for the Admiral's Men break off in October 1597, but it is less successful than before, making little more than £14 in total, with an average of 24s. per show.[12] The play clearly needed refurbishing, which it received in two steps when Ben Jonson was paid for writing additions for a revival in 1601 or 1602 by the Admiral's Men at their new Fortune playhouse (HD 182, 203).

Although Henslowe never refers to this play as *The Spanish Tragedy*, that identification "has never been disputed."[13] Likewise, the notion that the two sets of "Hieronimo" entries in the *Diary* (in 1592/3 and 1597) point to the *same* play has never been rigorously questioned, even though they are separated by a four-year gap and a switch in resident company. On the contrary, theatre historians often give the impression that the same Hieronimo play was

---

[11] Roslyn L. Knutson, "The Repertory," in *A New History of Early English Drama*, ed. John D. Cox and David Scott Kastan (Columbia University Press, 1997), 461–80, 467.

[12] For details, see *Henslowe's Diary*, ed. R. A. Foakes, 2nd ed. (Cambridge University Press, 2002), 17–19, 55–60 (subsequently cited as "HD").

[13] Lawrence Manley and Sally-Beth MacLean, *Lord Strange's Men and Their Plays* (Yale University Press, 2014), 78 (subsequently cited as "LSM"). That Philip Edwards in his standard Revels edition was particularly unrelenting in insisting that *The Spanish Tragedy* was an Admiral's Men's play doubtless shaped this consensus (Methuen, 1959; see esp. xxi–xxvii, lxvi–lxviii, 146–7).

continually staged at Henslowe's playhouse. Carol Chillington Rutter calls *The Spanish Tragedy* "a standby in the Rose repertoire since 1592."[14] Andrew Gurr claims that, for spectators at Henslowe's Rose, "seeing Alleyn as Hieronymo [*sic*], Tamburlaine, Barabbas, Faustus, or Muly Mahamet soon became a familiar experience," and that "*The Spanish Tragedy* continued to feature as a characteristic emblem of the Rose and the Fortune repertories until 1642."[15]

This traditional account has always been in tension with the documentary record. In fact, "seeing Alleyn as Hieronymo" may not have been an experience available to audiences at the Rose at all: there is no evidence that Edward Alleyn *ever* played the role. Despite Gurr's confident assertion that Alleyn's "favourite roles, Tamburlaine, Faustus, Barabbas, Hieronimo and Tamar Cham, all featured most strongly while he was in the company," the Admiral's Men did not stage a Hieronimo play for almost three years after moving to the Rose in 1594. And despite his claim that "Hieronimo, Tamburlaine and Faustus" were Alleyn's "most celebrated roles," *nobody* celebrated Alleyn's performance of Hieronimo in a form that left documentary traces.[16] Even if it were true that the actor took the lead in the 1597 "Joronymo" play (and we do not know if he did), witnessing him in the role would have been a short-lived experience for audiences: by the autumn of that year, Alleyn had "left playing."[17]

The emergence of Shakespeare as the author of the revisions, probably undertaken between 1596 and 1599, throws the orthodox narrative into disarray. That a playwright who was as integral a member of another company as Shakespeare should be doing patchwork for the Admiral's Men during those years, while perhaps not unthinkable, is without documented parallel. On closer examination, though, the attribution scholars'

---

[14] Carol Chillington Rutter, *Documents of the Rose Playhouse*, rev. ed. (Manchester University Press, 1999), 108.

[15] Andrew Gurr, *Shakespeare's Opposites: The Admiral's Company, 1594–1625* (Cambridge University Press, 2009), 49, 188.

[16] Ibid., 171.

[17] On Alleyn's temporary retirement, see S. P. Cerasano, "Edward Alleyn's 'Retirement' 1597–1600," *Medieval and Renaissance Drama in England* 10 (1998): 98–112.

findings conform with other theatre-historical evidence, some long-known but ignored, some newly relevant, that suggests that Henslowe's records are not as unambiguous as the received narrative implies – and that there are no firm connections between the Admiral's Men and *The Spanish Tragedy*.

I discuss this evidence in detail in subsequent sections, but here is Exhibit A: whereas no one mentioned Alleyn as Hieronimo, Richard Burbage, emerging in the late 1590s as the Chamberlain's Men's most famous actor, was repeatedly identified with the role of Hieronimo in contemporary sources. The part is one of four mentioned in a manuscript elegy written shortly after Burbage's death in 1619: "young Hamlet, old Hieronimo,/ Kind Lear, the grieved Moor, and more beside,/That liv'd in him, have now forever died."[18] Eighteen years earlier, shortly after Shakespeare wrote his additions, the second part of *Return from Parnassus*, a Cambridge University play, featured Burbage as a character who instructs a student actor how to play a line from *The Spanish Tragedy*: "I thinke your voice would serue for *Hieronimo*, obserue how I act it and then imitate mee."[19] And almost twenty years after Burbage's death, the association remained nearly proverbial. In his play *Wit's Triumvirate*, written for court performance in 1635, William Cavendish, the well-informed amateur playwright, describes the verse eruptions to which one of the characters is prone as "so lowd and acting as if *Burbedge's* soule newly reuiu'd *Hamlett*, & *Jeronimo* again, or *Allen*, *Tamburlayne*."[20] Three specific references to an actor playing a role may not seem like much, but they constitute the strongest

---

[18] Huntington Library HM 198, transcribed and modernized in Glynne Wickham, Herbert Berry, and William Ingram, eds., *English Professional Theatre, 1530–1660* (Cambridge University Press, 2000) (subsequently cited as "EPT"), 181–83, 182.

[19] *The Three Parnassus Plays (1598–1601)*, ed. J. B. Leishman (Nicholson and Watson, 1949), 341 (ll. 1803–5).

[20] Quoted in Samuel Schoenbaum, "*Wit's Triumvirate*: A Caroline Comedy Recovered," *Studies in English Literature, 1500–1900* 4 (1964): 227–37, 236. On Cavendish's authorship and his connections to early modern playwrights, see Tom Rutter, "The Cavendishes and Ben Jonson," *A Companion to the Cavendishes*, ed. Lisa Hopkins and Tom Rutter (Arc Humanities Press, 2020), 107–25, 115–17.

evidence of this kind we have for *any* part or performer.[21] To early modern theatregoers, certainly by the turn of the seventeenth century, Alleyn *was* Tamburlaine – and Burbage *was* Hieronimo.

The company with which Burbage was affiliated from 1594 to his death is also associated with *The Spanish Tragedy* in contemporary references and allusions, as I show in detail in Sections 3 and 5. In 1604, shortly after coming under royal patronage as the King's Men, the company itself laid claim to a Hieronimo play in John Webster's metatheatrical "Induction" to *The Malcontent*. There, a patron played by company sharer William Sly wonders why the King's Men would stage Marston's play, even though it was ostensibly owned by the Children of the Queen's Revels. Henry Condell, playing himself, responds, "Why not Malevole in folio with us, as Jeronimo in decimo-sexto with them? They taught us a name for our play: we call it, *One for Another*."[22] Adapting and staging *The Malcontent* is expressly framed as retaliation for the Children's appropriation of a Hieronimo play. Although Condell's us-vs.-them logic might simply reflect general rivalry between adult and boy companies, "*One for Another*" sounds rather like specific payback: the Children stole from the King's Men, and the King's Men stole back in turn.[23]

Given these explicit references, scholars have previously allowed for the possibility that *The Spanish Tragedy* made it into the Chamberlain's or King's Men's repertory at some point but have still been reluctant to contemplate the idea that the play never belonged to the Admiral's Men in the first place. Instead, the connection with Alleyn and the Admiral's Men is treated as beyond doubt, the link to Burbage and the Chamberlain's/King's Men as tenuous and difficult to explain.[24] Thus, the editors of the

---

[21] I have discussed the limited information about casting in the period in "A Sharers' Repertory," *Rethinking Theatrical Documents in Shakespeare's England*, ed. Tiffany Stern (Bloomsbury Arden Shakespeare, 2020), 33–51.

[22] John Marston, *The Malcontent*, ed. W. David Kay, New Mermaids (A & C Black, 1998), 12–13 (Induction 75–9).

[23] For arguments on either side, see Vickers, "Shakespeare's Additions," 17.

[24] Edwards simply dismisses all references to Burbage playing Hieronimo as "mistakes" (Revels edition, 147).

recent *Arden Early Modern Drama* edition of *The Spanish Tragedy* assert that "Hieronimo was played by some of the leading actors of the time, *certainly* by Edward Alleyn and *possibly* by Richard Burbage" – a statement that inverts what the evidence supports.[25] Dutton thinks *The Spanish Tragedy* "is securely with the Admiral's Men from 1597 and they did pay Ben Jonson quite a bit for 'additions to *Hieronimo*' in 1601/2" (Dutton 116n32). S. P. Cerasano sees "the persistence of *Jeronimo* in the repertory of the Admiral's Men through the middle of 1597" as evidence of Alleyn's connection to the play (even though "Jeronimo" did *not* persist in that repertory, as noted: it suddenly appeared in it after three years).[26] But how reliable is the conventional identification of that 1597 play as *The Spanish Tragedy?* Not only is there no evidence that Edward Alleyn played Hieronimo; there is also no evidence that the text behind the Admiral's Men's "Joronymo" was Kyd's play.[27] In fact, Henslowe's "ne" marker attached to the first appearance of that title suggests something else: that this was not the old *Spanish Tragedy*, but a new play based on the Hieronimo character. Discovering that Shakespeare wrote additions for Kyd's play in the late 1590s should now allow us to take Henslowe seriously. Doing so, as I show in detail in Sections 1 and 2, means concluding that *The Spanish Tragedy* was no longer performed at the Rose after Strange's Men left in January 1593, but instead entered the Chamberlain's Men's repertory when most of the Strange's sharers founded that new company.

---

[25] *The Spanish Tragedy*, ed. Clara Calvo and Jesús Tronch (Bloomsbury Arden Shakespeare, 2013), 61; my italics. All parenthetical references to *The Spanish Tragedy* will be to this edition.

[26] S. P. Cerasano, "Edward Alleyn, the New Model Actor, and the Rise of the Celebrity in the 1590s," *Medieval and Renaissance Drama in England* 18 (2005): 47–58, 48.

[27] For convenience's sake, I will refer to the Strange's Men's play as "Jeronymo" (the most frequent spelling) and to the Admiral's Men's as "Joronymo" (the more frequent spelling in this second set of records). Henslowe uses both spellings for both companies, and I don't believe the distinction has evidentiary value.

The following argument falls into two parts. Sections 1 and 2 address fundamental questions of theatre historical interpretation. In the first, I reconsider Henslowe's use of the tag "ne," and discuss what such a rereading might tell us about questions of newness, revival, and revision in the early modern theatre. In the second, I propose that many early modern play titles stood for clusters of plays spread across company repertories and identify the various *Hamlet* versions as well as the two *Shrew* plays as remnants of two such clusters. The argument then turns to a detailed discussion of *The Spanish Tragedy*'s theatrical contexts, locating it first in a complex of plays about Hieronimo, most of which are lost (Section 3), and finally, in the repertory of the Chamberlain's/King's Men, where its presence enables new readings of *Poetaster* and *The Alchemist*, which I offer as case studies (Section 5). Section 4 constitutes an interlude drawing on my previous arguments to rethink Jonson's early career as an actor, most notoriously in a version of the Hieronimo story. The epilogue traces the afterlife of *The Spanish Tragedy* in Restoration literary historiography, where we might encounter the long-lost author of one of the Hieronimo plays.

1 Ne Problem

When Philip Henslowe recorded the first performance of "Joronymo" by the Admiral's Men on 7 January 1597, he marked the entry "ne" – an annotation found next to fifty-two entries before this one, and next to sixty-five performances in total. If it were not for Malone's early transcription of the "Diary," though, the "ne" marker might have been missed by the document's modern editors. As W. W. Greg notes, "In this entry the *ne* has been carefully erased with a knife" (Greg 1.xlv), an observation that nevertheless did not lead him to restore the reading in the main text of his edition. Greg demonstrates that the culprit was almost certainly the notorious scholar-forger John Payne Collier, who produced a transcript for the Shakespeare Society in 1845. Why Collier? Erasing the "ne" strengthened an argument he wanted to make: that "Joronymo" was "probably a revival of the popular play called the Spanish Tragedy." Since Collier read Henslowe's "ne" as "invariably" marking "*the very day*" a play was "*acted for the first time*," this particular "ne" was evidence he needed to remove.[28]

Whether "Joronymo" was a new play or the old *Spanish Tragedy* appears to be primarily an editorial problem. From Collier on (assuming Greg was right in identifying his knife), the entry has been treated as a crux and an occasion for editorial emendation. In his own edition, Greg demonstrated that commentary, the editor's more elegant tool, is as powerful as blunt erasure. Rather than literally rewriting Henslowe's entry, he simply reinterpreted what "ne" may have meant. Restoring – at least in his comments – what his predecessor had "carefully" scratched out, Greg nevertheless retained Collier's reading: "Joronymo" in January 1597 indeed was *The Spanish Tragedy*, "performed as a new play," that is, old and "ne" at the same time (Greg 2.153–4). Greg's commentary, an interpretative rather than literal reshaping of Henslowe's text, has stood essentially unchallenged for well over a century.

The basis for Greg's reading was the assumption that Henslowe's "ne" tag is more complicated than Collier allowed when he glossed it as simply "the first two letters of the word *new*."[29] E. K. Chambers summarized the contrary position he and Greg both adopted: "it is evident that some of the plays marked 'ne' by Henslowe cannot have been new in the fullest sense."[30] In 1908, Greg gave a comprehensive list of what exactly "ne" meant:

(i)   that the play was new to the stage and had never before been acted;
(ii) that it was new to the company, but had been previously represented by some other body;
(iii) that it was new in its particular form, having received alterations since it was last acted. (Greg 2.148)

Such an elaborate gloss of a two-letter tag suggests a high degree of variance between the many instances of "ne"-marked entries in Henslowe. This is misleading, however. Eighty-eight per cent of those titles pose no challenge

---

[28] *The Diary of Philip Henslowe: From 1591 to 1609*, ed. John Payne Collier (Shakespeare Society), 1845, 84, xvii.

[29] Collier, *Diary*, xvii.

[30] E. K. Chambers, *The Elizabethan Stage* (Clarendon, 1923), 4 vols., vol. 2, 145 (subsequently cited as "ES").

to reading "ne" as "new." Of the sixty-five "ne" entries, fifty-seven were most likely new plays; at least they are not mentioned anywhere else before their first appearance in Henslowe's lists. We can presume that the many new playbooks whose purchase Henslowe records once his accounting of daily receipts breaks off would also have been entered as "ne" upon their first performance. Greg's first category thus seems to encompass almost *all* the appearances of the tag in the "Diary."

Only eight "ne" entries across the repertories of four companies performing at the Rose are at all challenging:

23 Jan 1594	titus & ondronicus	£3 8s.	Sussex's Men (HD 21)
11 Feb 1595	the frenshe Comodey	£2 10s.	Admiral's Men (HD 27)
6 May 1596	tambercame	£2 7s.	Admiral's Men (HD 36)
11 June 1596	2 p[ar]te of tambercame	£3	Admiral's Men (HD 47)
7 Jan 1597	Joronymo	£3	Admiral's Men (HD 55)
14 Jan 1597	elexsander & lodwicke	£2 15s.	Admiral's Men (HD 56)
11 Feb 1597	elexsander & lodwecke	£3 5s.	Admiral's Men (HD 56)
18 Apr 1597	a frenshe comodey	£2	Admiral's Men (HD 57)

Greg's second and third categories might, in theory, apply to all eight. But not all appear problematic for the same reasons. Two pairs (the two "French Comedies" and the two appearances of "Alexander and Lodowick") are repeat "ne"s within the repertory of the same company. Three other entries look like plays previously performed at the Rose by a different company: the two parts of "Tamar Cham" (the modern rendition of Henslowe's idiosyncratic "tambercame") and "Joronymo" correspond to titles in the repertory of Strange's Men in 1592/3. And finally, there is *Titus Andronicus* – the entry that really drives much of the "ne" scepticism, since few scholars have been willing to accept that Shakespeare and Peele's play could have been written as late as the winter of 1593/4. If it were not for the problem that record poses for the chronology of Shakespeare's playwriting, it is unlikely that anyone would ever have questioned that "ne" meant "new" for "titus & ondronicus."

Greg's second category, plays previously performed but new to the company concerned, can be dismissed right away, since it cannot be reconciled with the facts of the "Diary." Henslowe does *not* normally tag plays as "ne" if they reappear after previously having been staged by "some other body" using his theatre. Examples are readily available:

- *The Jew of Malta* was performed by Strange's Men, Sussex's Men, and the Admiral's Men, but is never marked "ne," although it must surely have been new to at least one of those companies.
- *The Massacre at Paris* (by scholarly consensus, the play behind Henslowe's "the tragedy of the gvyes") is "ne" on its first and only appearance during Strange's Men's residency, on 30 January 1593, but not when it next shows up, in the repertory of the Admiral's Men, on 19 June 1594.
- "The Ranger's Comedy"[31] is first entered as either Sussex's or the Queen's Men's property on 2 April 1594, and not marked "ne" (even though both companies were, as far as we know, new to the Rose); when it next appears, with the Admiral's Men on 15 May 1594, it still isn't "ne."
- *Titus Andronicus* is "ne" when performed by Sussex's Men on 23 January 1594, but not when staged by the Admiral's or (more likely) Chamberlain's Men on 5 June 1594.

In fact, Greg's second category seems designed to accommodate just three entries: the two parts of "Tamar Cham" and "Jeronimo." Those titles all also appear in the lists for Strange's Men in 1592–3, "1 Tamar Cham" as an old play that was performed three times in May and June 1592, and once in January 1593; "2 Tamar Cham" as a "ne" play staged twice in April and May 1592; and "Jeronymo" as an old play with thirteen performances from March to June that year, and another run of three from December 1592 to January 1593. A two-part "Tamar Cham" then enters the Admiral's Men's repertory towards the end of their second season at the Rose, with Part 1

---

[31] I cite titles of lost plays in quotation marks throughout and italicize those of texts that survive in print or manuscript.

introduced as "ne" on 6 May 1596, followed quickly by Part 2, also "ne," on 11 June. In their next season, they first perform "Jeronimo," as "ne," on 7 January 1597. Since other plays could switch from one company to another without being marked "ne," though, it is unlikely that these apparent transfers were the reason for the tags. The three entries will therefore need to be examined as possible "newly revised" plays.

The "newly revised" category, however, stands on similarly shaky ground. The only other entries to which it might apply are the two "French Comedies," staged by the Admiral's Men as "ne" two years apart from each other; and "Alexander and Lodowick," a lost play marked "ne" twice in a row, with less than a month between those performances. However, no evidence exists that the two "French Comedies" were revised before their "ne" stagings. "Alexander and Lodowick," a play that is an exception in more ways than one (as I detail below), might have been – but if so, in an unusual fashion.

Let me now address the putatively problematic "ne" plays one by one, to demonstrate that the assertion that they "cannot have been new in the fullest sense" rests in all cases on prior assumptions that lack strong evidentiary support.

The Titus *Question*

The "ne" tag for *Titus Andronicus* is not contradicted by anything in the "Diary," but challenges a long-standing majority conviction that Shakespeare could not possibly still have been writing this kind of drama as late as January 1594. Jonathan Bate took up an outlier position in his Arden Third Series edition when he accepted Henslowe's text. Since he oddly follows orthodoxy in seeing *other* "ne"s as more questionable, however, he is forced to invent a change in Henslowe's recording practices: "it was only from late 1595 onwards that 'ne' was occasionally written beside an older play that was either newly revised or new to the company performing it."[32]

---

[32] *Titus Andronicus*, ed. Bate, Arden Shakespeare Third Series (Routledge, 1995), 70fn.

Other scholars have mobilized the idea that the tag could mean "newly revised" to suggest that the version of *Titus* in January 1594 was either a mixture of old (by Peele) and new (by Shakespeare) or not the text published later that year (and subsequently in the 1623 Folio), which, they argue, must have been an older version.[33] *Titus Andronicus* is an exceptionally complicated case because it emerges during a period of extreme commercial upheaval and it is difficult to determine which company owned the play when. However, there might be a straightforward explanation for its "ne" tag: "new," in the theatre, does not necessarily mean "newly written."

By the time Sussex's Men began their six-week stint at the Rose in late December 1593, the theatres in London had suffered through a closure of eighteen months broken only by a few weeks of theatrical activity from late December 1592 to January 1593. A play written in early 1592 might never have made it to performance before the London playhouses were shuttered in late June, and a company would have been unlikely to invest in mounting a new play while on tour after that date. What is more, the text contains hints that *Titus* was written at some remove from specific performance prospects. Rory Loughnane has discussed the challenges of understanding the stage space envisaged in the first scene of *Titus Andronicus*, arguing that they may arise from Shakespeare adding stage directions to Peele's original version of the scene.[34] If so, we could perhaps imagine the scene first being written without a specific playhouse in mind *because none was available*, and subsequently being hastily revised close to its first performance for the stage at the Rose. The *New Oxford Shakespeare* editors' conclusion that the play should chronologically be associated with Shakespeare's "pre-plague plays" would also support such a scenario.[35]

---

[33] For a detailed analysis of scholarly attempts to account for the *Titus* "ne," see Terence Schoone-Jongen, *Shakespeare's Companies: William Shakespeare's Early Career and the Acting Companies, 1577–1594* (Ashgate, 2008), 151–7.

[34] Rory Loughnane, "Re-editing Non-Shakespeare for the Modern Reader: The Murder of Mutius in *Titus Andronicus*," *Review of English Studies* 68 (2016): 268–95, 291–2.

[35] Gary Taylor and Rory Loughnane, "The Canon and Chronology of Shakespeare's Works," in *New Oxford Shakespeare: Authorship Companion*, 417–602, 493.

Given the instability of the London theatre market after June 1592, some of the plays that appeared as "ne" once the situation settled down in the second half of 1594 were very likely the product of those disrupted two years; some may have been ready to go into production when the playhouses shut down. That they were written years earlier, however, did not make those plays anything other than *theatrically* new when they eventually appeared on stage in 1594: not merely new to a particular company, not just new in a particular venue, not even new only to London audiences, but staged publicly for the very first time. There is no reason *Titus Andronicus* could not have been one of those plays – begun (and perhaps abandoned?) by Peele and taken over by Shakespeare before the June 1592 closure, or in the months directly afterwards, maybe even completed then in anticipation of an imminent reopening of the playhouses. Nor is there any reason the play would not have been ignored for a year, perhaps as much as eighteen months, with no company able or willing to buy the book or invest in costumes and props. It is telling that it took Sussex's Men almost a month before they staged this, their first and only "ne" play at the Rose. The ten plays they put on before *Titus* were all new to Henslowe's records but not new to the London stage, or so the absence of "ne" markers implies. Even so, they yielded remarkably high revenues, presumably because London's playgoers were keen to return to the theatre. After their first three performances brought in more than £3 each, a run rarely equaled elsewhere in the "Diary," the company may have assumed themselves on sound enough footing to think about investing in their first new production; twenty-five days later, *Titus Andronicus* premiered. Sussex's Men could not have anticipated that less than two weeks later, the playhouses would be shut down once again – and that their third performance of *Titus* on 6 February 1594 would also be the last time they staged the play in London.[36]

---

[36] Scholars have often held that the other two companies named on the title page of *Titus*'s first quarto, printed sometime in 1594 (Derby's Men and Pembroke's Men), must have performed the play *before* Sussex's Men because that is the order in which the quarto lists them. I have argued elsewhere that reading the sequence of companies as arranged alphabetically is equally warranted, and that Pembroke's Men probably owned the play at least until 1596; see "Three's

French Comedies

The most obviously challenging appearances of "ne" in the "Diary" are those attached to two titles that the Admiral's Men seem to have performed before. Of those, "Alexander and Lodowick" poses a particularly interesting problem. The other apparent duplicate entry may be considerably less interesting – and as likely as not poses no challenge at all. As Martin Wiggins writes, "it is possible for more than one comedy to be set in France."[37] "[T]he frenshe Comedey," "ne" on 11 February 1595, may simply be a *different* play from the equally blandly titled "a frenshe comodey," tagged "ne" on 18 April 1597.[38] Before disappearing from Henslowe's lists after a mere six performances, the earlier play was last staged on 24 June 1595, making a healthy 30s. (with revenues, which were always higher on holidays, likely boosted by the Midsummer Day scheduling). Takings throughout its run were undistinguished: the average Admiral's Men "ne" play made 35s. over its first six outings in Henslowe's records, whilst "The French Comedy" yielded just under 31s. Revenues were not so catastrophically low, though, that the decision to drop it from the repertory so soon is easily explained. Almost as much of a puzzle is the very low income "A French Comedy" yielded Henslowe when it (re)appears in his records, "ne" once more, in 1597 – at a mere £2, the fifth lowest income from a "ne" play in the "Diary," a lacklustre opening that was followed by a relatively long run of ten more performances with similarly subpar takings. That does not mean that the play was not new,

---

Company: Alternative Histories of London's Theatres in the 1590s," *Shakespeare Survey* 65 (2012): 269–89, 281–3.

[37] Martin Wiggins and Catherine Richardson, *British Drama 1533–1642: A Catalogue* (Oxford University Press, 2011–18), 9 vols., entry #1066 (subsequently cited as "BDC" and by entry number).

[38] I am using the definite and indefinite articles here to distinguish the two sets of entries. Henslowe *may* have done so as well: in the first set of records, the play is always "*the* frenshe comedey"; in the second run of entries, the play is first "*a* frenche comedey," then simply "french" – or "frenshe" – "comodey" on nine other occasions, with one more "*a* frenshe comedey" in the middle of the run, but never "the" (HD 27–8, 30, 57–9).

though: throughout 1597, Henslowe registered much lower receipts for "ne" titles than in previous years, with only "Alexander and Lodowick" and "Joronymo" earning £3 or more on opening day. By contrast, twenty other titles made at least that much in the Admiral's Men's two previous seasons.[39] However, if "A French Comedy" *was* a revival, it is unclear why a gap of just twenty-two months would have been enough to earn it the "ne" tag. Other plays were not treated analogously: "Belin Dun," revived for a single performance on 11 July 1596 after a twenty-month absence, was not specially marked on that occasion, nor when it returned for a run of seven shows on 31 March 1597 (HD 48, 57).

Revision does not offer itself as a likely scenario. When "The French Comedy" left the repertory two years earlier, it had not yet been performed very often, and its revenues signal neither great popularity nor waning impact. The play, the records suggest, was as unremarkable as the title Henslowe uses for it. Everything we know about the Admiral's Men's habits implies that they tended to avoid revisions, reserved them primarily for court performances, and otherwise limited them mostly to plays at least a decade old and with long-established track records. When faced with the decision of whether to invest the full £6 a new play usually cost or paying between £2 and £4 for revisions and additions, the company rarely went the latter route: as Knutson has argued, they "did not see the payment for revisions to accompany a revival as a commercially necessary or profitable venture."[40] The only documented exceptions are *Doctor Faustus* and "Joronymo": both received expensive additions in 1601 and 1602. In this context, a script with as little theatrical exposure and as limited previous success as "The French Comedy" does not look like a candidate for a

---

[39] See Roslyn L. Knutson, "Henslowe's Diary and the Economics of Play Revision for Revival, 1592–1603," *Theatre Research International* 10 (1985): 1–18, 8–11, for a discussion of the low receipts for new plays in 1597 and the company's commercially unsuccessful strategy of quickly reviving old titles to counter a downward trend in revenues.

[40] Knutson, "Economics of Play Revision," 11. See also Dutton 98–137, demonstrating just how few documented examples exist of plays that were substantially revised or augmented in the period.

revival with revisions. Thus, reading the "ne" tag straightforwardly as "new" in this case makes more sense than the alternative scenarios.

"Alexander and Lodowick": The Key to "Ne"

The case of "Alexander and Lodowick" is as interesting as that of the "French Comedies" is unexceptional. There is no real doubt that it was performed as "ne" twice in a row. It may be that Henslowe simply made a mistake when writing that second "ne," but if we aim to read (rather than correct) the "Diary," we should assume that the tags are not erroneous. Why might that be? That both entries refer to the same work seems indisputable, given their proximity. But the double "ne" is not the only thing worth noting about "Alexander and Lodowick." For one, there is an unusually long break between the two performances. Only one other "ne" play in the entire "Diary" had to wait as long for its second staging: "Palamon and Arcite" opened on 17 September 1594 and was not seen again until 16 October. But unlike "Alexander and Lodowick," that play fared indifferently on its first outing, with £2 11s. of takings, and much worse on its second performance (£1 7s.) (HD 24). By contrast, "Alexander and Lodowick" was the second-best "ne" opening of the 1596/97 season (£2 15s.) to that point, and its second "ne" performance improved on that, setting the season's high mark for revenues (£3 5s.). More remarkably still, the play was then *immediately* scheduled again, the first time since April 1595 the Admiral's Men had offered the same title on consecutive days.[41]

What, then, might this highly atypical play tell us about "ne"? It seems to me that the best explanation for its unusual record is an old one, first proposed by Foakes and Rickert in their 1961 edition of the "Diary": that "ne" means "newly licensed" and that, in the case of "Alexander and Lodowick," something went wrong, so that the play "had for some reason to be withdrawn and relicensed" (HD xxxv). Since they assume that "a revival, at least when substantial revision had been made," required a new license, their reading of "ne" leaves Greg's categories mostly intact. Even

---

[41] They had done so only once before, when they staged "The Wise Man of West Chester," the greatest commercial success in the "Diary," on 25 and 26 April 1595 (HD 28).

his second category – which, as I've argued, is probably a chimera – would be compatible with Foakes and Rickert's interpretation, if, as Dutton has maintained, the Master of the Revels would not have allowed plays "to change hands without [a] formal agreement" (Dutton 116n32), and if that process involved a new license and fee. However, their explanation identifies licensing as an underlying common denominator that crucially begins to explain why Henslowe would have highlighted those performances. The link between "ne" and licenses is almost confirmed by an observation first offered by Carol Chillington in a 1980 footnote: that Henslowe's note "17 p from hence licensed" on 10 March 1595 (HD 28) meant that seventeen plays had been licensed up to that point – and that the Admiral's Men had performed precisely seventeen "ne" plays by then, from "Belin Dun" on 8 June 1594 to "Seleo and Olympo" on 5 March.[42]

Licenses came at a cost: as we know from various entries later in the "Diary," Edmund Tilney charged 7s. per play. If Henslowe, who also paid the separate weekly licensing fee for his playhouse and thus had regular dealings with the Revels office, advanced fees for new plays on the company's behalf, that could explain why he recorded the occasions of such expenses. However, I think there is a better explanation, one that links the Master of the Revels' licensing fee with what has long been identified as the most noteworthy aspect of "ne" performances: that their revenues were "always high" (HD xxxiv). On average, the opening of a "ne" play yielded £2 12s., whereas plays that are not so marked generated an average of just under £2 1s. on their (re)opening days.

Part of the explanation must be that new plays were inherently attractive. The traveller Samuel Kiechel wrote in 1585 that playhouses drew especially large crowds "when they act anything new," and "double prices are charged" for admissions on those occasions (quoted in ES 2.358). It is unclear whether this pricing practice continued after the 1580s, but the opening day crush became near-proverbial. Dekker, for instance, referred

---

[42] Carol Chillington, "Playwrights at Work: Henslowe's, Not Shakespeare's, Book of Sir Thomas More," *English Literary Renaissance* 10 (1980): 439–79, 446n9; see also Neil Carson, *A Companion to Henslowe's Diary* (Cambridge University Press, 1988), 17.

to "crowding (as if it had been a new play)."[43] But higher receipts on "ne" days cannot simply reflect doubled prices of admission. For one, revenue differences between first performances of new and old plays are insufficiently large: even the highest earning "ne" opening for the Admiral's Men ("1 Hercules" on 7 May 1595, £3 13s.) did not yield double the average opening income of old plays (£2 1s.). Knutson has also pointed out that admission was charged "at the playhouse door," where everyone entering the theatre paid their penny, no matter whether they stood in the yard or paid more to access the galleries once inside the playhouse. She surmises that the doubled price would have been levied at the door (2p rather than 1p), and not also "at the gallery entrance from which Henslowe's receipts were drawn" – and I agree that Henslowe's receipts do not show the massive impact doubled gallery admissions fees would have produced.[44] In any case, not *all* "ne" openings generated huge revenues; in fact, some of the highest-grossing performances in the "Diary" are the opening days of well-known old plays (*Doctor Faustus* on 30 September 1594, for instance, earned £3 12s.). And other extremely high-earning performances fall later in the run of some plays: the fifth outing of "The Wise Man of West Chester" made £3 6s. and the sixth performance of "The Comedy of Humours" £3 10s. The primary driver of revenues was evidently audience demand, not increased admissions prices. It is equally clear, by the same token, that the galleries at the Rose were often half-full at best.

That said, even the figures recorded for worst-earning "ne" openings are at least as high as the old-play average. Something in how new-play openings were logged by Henslowe seemed to guarantee a fairly high minimum income floor. The solution, I think, lies in a long-ignored suggestion Neil Carson proffered in 1988: that Henslowe did not record his own share of the daily gallery receipts, but rather the half he owed, or paid, to the players. As Carson notes, such an interpretation would match Henslowe's "non-theatrical accounts, which are mostly statements of

---

[43] Quoted in Ann Jennalie Cook, *The Privileged Playgoers of Shakespeare's London, 1576–1642* (Princeton University Press, 1981), 193n67.

[44] Roslyn L. Knutson, *The Repertory of Shakespeare's Company, 1594–1613* (University of Arkansas Press, 1991), 25.

expenditures rather than income."[45] The idea was not received favourably in reviews of Carson's book. Remington P. Patterson dismissed it, without further explanation, as "possible, perhaps, but not very clear, and far from likely"; Roslyn Knutson, more reasonably, wondered what the significance of the claim was: "if the sums are indeed half of the galleries, what difference does it make whose half?"[46] I would suggest that the difference between Henslowe receiving half the takings *from* the players and Henslowe collecting all the gallery income and then returning half of it *to* the players comes into focus on "ne" days. Foakes and Rickert argued that "the company would need increased takings" for new plays "to recoup the sum spent on licensing," and thus increased the admissions fee (HD xxxiv–v). But what if instead, on "ne" days the players, having paid the license, received more than their usual moiety of the gallery takings from Henslowe? The sums involved match this scenario much more closely than the doubled-admissions theory does. If Henslowe had agreed to always deduct 7s. from his half of the gallery revenues on "ne" days and add them to the share he owed the players, that would account for 64 per cent of the 11s. difference between the average income from "ne" openings and from the first performances of old plays; the remaining 36 per cent can be accounted for as simply the difference in inherent audience interest.

Such a reading of the "ne" figures does not *require* that we accept Carson's interpretation: if we instead assume that Henslowe himself paid the licensing fees, the 7s. difference could also be the reimbursement he received from the players every time a newly licensed play opened. But I favour the scenario just outlined for three reasons. Firstly, the "Diary" contains multiple references to play licenses being paid *by the company*: Henslowe records lending them money for such expenses on 15 January and 28 March 1598, for instance. These are not *Henslowe's* expenses, but charges to the Admiral's Men's account, recorded alongside similar loans for payments for scripts and costumes (HD 86, 88).[47]

---

[45] Carson, *Companion*, 21.

[46] Patterson, review in *Medieval and Renaissance Drama in England* 6 (1993), 273–8, 275; Knutson, review in *Shakespeare Bulletin* 6 (1988): 46–7, 46.

[47] On two later occasions in 1600, however, he records two payments for licenses he made directly to the Master of the Revels without explicitly stating that these were made "at the appointment" of the company (HD 134).

Secondly, it makes sense to me that Henslowe would highlight occasions on which he needed to deviate from his established practice of retaining half the gallery incomes, whereas it is unclear to me why he would need to remind himself why he received an unusually large daily payment on a specific day. Thirdly, if on those days, *Henslowe* rather than the players had to do something he did not normally do, we might finally have a plausible explanation for what exactly "ne" might stand for. "Ne," after all, is an odd abbreviation for "new," and Henslowe does not use it anywhere else. Alternative explanations, such as Malone's "new enterlude" or Foakes's "newly entered" are also unconvincing: "entered" is Stationers' language, not Revels Office terminology, and "enterlude" is not used elsewhere in the "Diary." Henslowe in any event does not typically use acronyms; he normally abbreviates by running the first and last letter of a word together, as in "Rd" for "received."[48] Instead, as David McInnis has suggested to me, the tag might be the Latin "ne," used loosely by Henslowe to mean something like "do not" – in this case, "do not retain your full moiety."[49]

Returning now to "Alexander and Lodowick," we can bring the narrative of what may have happened into sharper focus. The play was new when first performed. Despite its immediate commercial success, the company refrained from staging the play again for almost a month, and, when they did, Henslowe marks it once more as newly licensed. The scenario that best explains these circumstances, to my mind, is a first performance that was not as egregiously offensive to the authorities as that of "The Isle of Dogs" by Pembroke's Men a few months later, but one that caused *someone* to take exception, even though the play had been licensed. As Dutton has recently suggested, the Master of the Revels may have treated plays that did not "self-evidently dea[l] with queasy topics" with less "detailed attention," and perhaps Tilney missed something in what was likely a script based on a bloody, but hardly topical, fairy-tale romance.[50] The problem must have been

---

[48] Greg 2.148; R. A. Foakes, "The Discovery of the Rose Theatre: Some Implication," *Shakespeare Survey* 43 (1991): 141–8, 147.

[49] McInnis, personal communication, 19 July 2022.

[50] Dutton, *Mastering the Revels: The Regulation and Censorship of Early Modern Drama*, 2nd ed. (Oxford University Press, 2022), 4. For the probable source of the play,

more severe than just a few objectionable lines, since the required revisions took time and were extensive enough to necessitate a new license. If Tilney's practice at all anticipated his successor Sir Henry Herbert's approach, fees for relicensing were only charged if "perusal" of the text was required. We know of at least one case where Herbert called in an already licensed play, Shirley's *The Martyred Soldier*, when he heard that the players did not "observe" the "reformations" he had demanded; he then levied his fee again "to peruse itt."[51] Something like this may have happened with "Alexander and Lodowick," leading to the two charges. Presumably all this back and forth gave the play some notoriety: its return to the stage yielded the highest gallery revenues of any "ne" opening in the 1596/7 season, and it became the most-performed play that season, which must have gone some way towards making up for the additional costs of revisions and a second license.

The "Tamar Cham"s and the Question of Revision

If my account of "Alexander and Lodowick" is at least plausible, the play, on its second appearance, fits a modified version of Greg's third category: newly licensed because of revisions. If revisions did in fact always call for a new license, that created an additional "strong economic disincentive against the practice," as Gabriel Egan has argued, building on Knutson's research.[52] Egan also notes, though, that Masters of the Revels before Herbert may not have insisted on relicensing revised scripts; Herbert himself thought his predecessors allowed "poets" to take "greater liberty than is allowed them by mee." He certainly felt that previously licensed

see Roslyn Knutson, David McInnis, and Matthew Steggle, eds., *Lost Plays Database* (Folger Shakespeare Library, 2009–), https://lostplays.folger.edu/Alexander_and_Lodowick (subsequent entries cited by URL).

[51] N. W. Bawcutt, ed., *The Control and Censorship of Caroline Drama: The Records of Sir Henry Herbert, Master of the Revels 1623–73* (Clarendon, 1996), 143–4 (subsequently cited as "Bawcutt"). In this case, Herbert was incensed enough to make an example of the company. He did not release the play back to them but licensed it to a different company a few months later, charging his fee once more on that occasion.

[52] Gabriel Egan, "Early Modern Play Manuscripts and Their Licensing," https://gabrielegan.com/publications/Egan2013l.htm.

plays needed to be submitted to him for preapproval before they could be revived – a position Dutton describes as a "new policy," previous Masters' licenses having been "good indefinitely" (Dutton 154). Unless an old play had been altered, Herbert would not charge a fee for such new licenses; on numerous occasions, however, he did exact a payment, usually half as much as for a regular license, for reading additions ranging from "a scene" or "some alterations" to "a new act" or even "an old play, new written or furbished."[53] In a revealing entry, Herbert captures what at least some companies hoped to achieve by revising old scripts: "Received of old Cartwright for allowing the <Fortune> company to add scenes to an old play, and to give it out for a new one … £1 0 0" (Bawcutt 199).

Passing off an old text spruced up with a few new scenes as an entirely new play was presumably not the motivation for most revisions; it could hardly have worked with well-known classics such as *Doctor Faustus* or, indeed, *The Spanish Tragedy*. But old Cartwright's ploy supports Knutson, Egan, and Dutton's sense that revisions were not routine but specifically motivated: the Fortune company's goal in staging that old play was to save money. Rather than commission and license a new play, they found a forgotten text, paid someone to write new material for it, which would have been cheaper than a full new script, and only had to cover half of Herbert's usual licensing fee (by 1632, £2). If they could have got away with "giv[ing] it out for a new one" *without* revisions, they would presumably have done so. Oldness here is both a precondition for the stratagem and a slight liability: the play needed to be shelf-worn enough to have become unrecognizable, but it required sufficient refurbishment to disguise its actual age. Within those parameters, however, revision was the economically sensible choice.[54]

---

[53] See Bawcutt 153, 181, 168, 174.

[54] As far as can be determined, almost all additions Herbert lists were for old plays; Rowley's "Hymen's Holiday," one of the few we can date, was relicensed in 1633 (Bawcutt 181), when it was at least twenty-one years old (see https://lostplays. folger.edu/Hymen%27s_Holiday_or_Cupid%27s_Vagaries). The odd one out is an addition to Dekker and Massinger's *The Virgin Martyr*, recorded in July 1624, when the play *may* have been only four years old. However, that dating itself depends on an uncertain listing of an unusual charge of £2 from October

Turning to the remaining contested "ne" plays now, I should say, first, that we know nothing about their textual status: asserting that "Joronymo" and the two parts of "Tamar Cham" were marked "ne" because they had been revised and relicensed is little more than a convenient fiction. We do not know whether they were revised, nor if Tilney would have charged the players for revisions, nor if Henslowe would have granted the financial terms that I have argued "ne" denotes for performances incurring such additional charges. The case of "Alexander and Lodowick" does not provide a model for this scenario because it is such an obvious outlier. Neither, as I have argued, does it seem credible that those three plays fall into Greg's second category of plays marked "ne" because they switched company. Beyond the evidence I adduced earlier to show that this category is likely a chimera, it is a particularly poor fit for the "Tamar Cham" plays. Why? Because we know that one or both belonged to Edward Alleyn: the Admiral's Men bought the book for "Tamar Chan" from him on 2 October 1602 for 40s., the customary price for an old play (HD 205). Alleyn also owned *Massacre at Paris*, which he sold to the company in January 1602 (HD 187). One might want to argue that *Massacre* was not marked "ne" when it switched from Strange's Men to the Admiral's Men because it was owned by Alleyn, and the license therefore went with him. That is in fact a plausible argument, but if so, it would equally apply to "Tamar Cham," whose "ne" tags then become all the more puzzling.

If Greg's second category is ruled out altogether as a credible hypothesis, however, only three possibilities remain: Henslowe made mistakes and none of those three plays should have been "ne" at all (an all too convenient assumption); the three plays were new; or the three plays were revised, and "ne" could mean "revised and relicensed." Why would we think that the "Tamar Cham" plays were revised? In the case of "Joronymo," at least one could argue that, if the entry refers to *The Spanish Tragedy*, the play was relatively old, and, after a long theatrical career, might have been due a refurbishment. The "Tamar Cham" plays do not at all fit that mould, however.

1620 for "new reforming the *Virgin Martyr* for the Red Bull," which may not refer to a new play's first performance (Bawcutt 153, 135).

A two-part "Tamar Cham" was staged by Strange's Men during their residency at the Rose, beginning with a "ne" performance of "the second p[ar]te of tamber came" on 28 April 1592. Scholars have routinely assumed that the Admiral's Men's plays listed under the same title are identical to the ones put on by Strange's Men. That supposition *might* find support in Alleyn's ownership of at least one of the two parts. (Henslowe's record of the sale is ambiguous enough that it is unclear whether the two parts counted as one book.) Alleyn, in this scenario, brought the play with him when he reunited with the Admiral's company, just as he did with *Massacre at Paris*. When Part I of "Tamar Cham" was first staged is uncertain, since its initial appearance in the "Diary" is not marked "ne." Some judicious speculation is possible, however. Strange's Men may have commissioned the play(s) to copy Alleyn's success in a similar role, though one he could no longer perform: Tamburlaine. Henslowe's records suggest that Marlowe's two-part play, along with *Doctor Faustus*, always belonged to the Admiral's Men, and that Alleyn lost access to them when he temporarily left his old company. If "Tamar Cham" was a *Tamburlaine* replacement, we can probably date it to the end of 1591 at the earliest, since Alleyn and the Admiral's Men seem to have split at some point after May of that year.[55] But if Strange's Men were hoping for a new *Tamburlaine*, Henslowe's figures suggest a less impressive outcome. The "Tamar Cham" plays are among the least-performed titles in the company's repertory, with the second part only receiving a single outing after its reasonably successful opening (£3 4s., significantly less than four of the seven "ne" plays in their records). The first part was on stage just three times in the 1592/3 season and came back for a single performance in January, when the company returned to the Rose briefly in the winter; it always yielded takings just above average.[56]

---

[55] Alleyn, his brother John, and James Tunstall, all Admiral's Men, were involved in the purchase of a cloak for £20 10s. on 6 May 1591, doubtless for the company's stock of costumes. Given this investment, it appears unlikely that Alleyn left the Admiral's Men immediately thereafter (Dulwich College Archive MS 1, Article 5, digitized at https://henslowe-alleyn.org.uk/catalogue/mss-1/article-005).

[56] The distinction between the parts is a little hazy. Henslowe lists two performances of Part 2 and four others without specifying the part. Knutson has argued

If the scholarly assumption that these plays moved with Alleyn to the Admiral's Men holds true, it is puzzling that they should have been revised so quickly, especially since they had hardly outstayed their welcome when Strange's Men staged them. Neither of the two parts was old when they (re) appear in Henslowe's records in 1596, and no matter how we read the 1592/ 3 records, the second part had hardly been performed at all. Neither play looks anything like a candidate for major revisions by 1596. In effect, these entries pose the same challenge as the two French Comedies: plays with near-identical titles, listed almost two years apart, both times as "ne." Why can the answer to the riddle not be the same in both cases: that these "ne" plays were in fact new? Such a hypothesis asks us to read Henslowe literally and to proceed from the assumption that whenever he wrote "ne," he meant the same thing. What follows, then, is that the Admiral's Men had two distinct, moderately successful comedies on a French theme in their repertory within two years; and that both Strange's Men and the Admiral's Men performed two-part plays about Tamar Cham, also almost two years apart. We know, for instance, that the Admiral's Men and the Chamberlain's Men staged plays about Henry V within two years of each other. Why would it be so difficult to believe that "Tamar Cham" is simply another instance of such cross-repertory duplication?

There is no need to abandon the argument that Strange's Men's "Tamar Cham" was meant as a *Tamburlaine* replacement. In fact, the introduction of the two "ne" plays about Tamar Cham into the Admiral's Men's repertory replicated that effect. Having reintroduced Alleyn as Tamburlaine at the end of August 1594, the company kept Marlowe's two plays in their repertory through May 1595, with a few sporadic performances later that year. After a six-month gap, they then brought back Alleyn in what may have been a similarly stage-strutting role in Part I of "Tamar Cham." We might even be tempted to speculate that Alleyn himself recognized that

that we should take him at his word and interprets those four entries as performances of "1 Tamar Cham," since Henslowe often omits the numeral when referring to the first of two parts ("Henslowe's Naming of Parts: Entries in the Diary for Tamar Cham, 1592–3, and Godfrey of Bulloigne, 1594–5," *Notes and Queries* 30 (1983): 157–60).

channeling this aspect of his actorly energies into more than one role of this type made commercial sense. As Henslowe's records show, having both sets of plays in their repertory ended up making good sense to the Admiral's Men, and not only in the short run. They both enjoyed a long stage life: inventories of the company's stock still record costume pieces for *Tamburlaine* in 1598/9, and "Tamar Cham" was certainly back on stage after the move to the newly built Fortune playhouse in 1601 (HD 320–2, 332–3). A performance of the first part between 1600 and 1603 is documented in a backstage "plot" naming Edward Alleyn in the title role; and in late 1602, the company considered the play of sufficiently lasting value to buy the playbook from Alleyn.[57] There is no indication, though, that "Tamar Cham" ever required revisions to remain stageworthy. Henslowe's records thus implicitly answer Martin Wiggins's question, "if the Admiral's Men already had *Tamburlaine*, why would they also need *Tamar Cham*?" (BDC #906): because rotating the two kept both sets of plays fresh enough to allow them passage to the status of classic, seemingly without any need for rewrites or additions.

The salient point here is this: the fact that a pair of "Tamar Cham" plays existed in the repertory of Strange's Men tells us nothing about the "Tamar Cham" plays in the repertory of the Admiral's Men. Henslowe's identification of the latter plays as "ne" when first performed can be taken at face value: there is no reason to assume and no evidence that suggests that these were revisions of older (but not very old) works.

Joronymo, Anew

I hope to have established by now a sense of dwindling probability that "ne" meant anything other than "a newly licensed play," and that in every instance but the highly atypical "Alexander and Lodowick," that meant "a new play."

The only case remaining is "Joronymo." As I have outlined in the Introduction, there is no basis whatsoever for connecting *The Spanish*

---

[57] "Plots" were single-sheet breakdowns of plays, showing entrances and major props; they usually also specify casting, especially for actors playing multiple roles. The "1 Tamar Cham" plot survives only in the form of a transcript published in 1803; six others are extant in manuscript.

Tragedy with the Admiral's Men except for the entry in Henslowe's "Diary." But even that, as should be clear by now, is an overstatement. To put it plainly: we can only connect the 1597 "Joronymo" to *The Spanish Tragedy* if we ignore or explain away what Henslowe's entry says, thereby completing Collier's act of erasure by different scholarly means. To do so, we need to think of Henslowe as simultaneously devoid of ambiguity (he never uses the same title for different plays, a flatly counterfactual notion, as I will show in Section 2) and happily ambiguous in his use of the supposedly mystifying "ne." But "ne" is only puzzling if we presume to know more than Henslowe tells us: if we assume that *Titus* cannot have been first staged in 1594, that the Admiral's Men did not have their own "Tamar Cham" plays, or that there was only one tragedy about Hieronimo.

Perhaps unsurprisingly, ignoring Henslowe creates all kinds of complications. If "Joronymo" was in fact *The Spanish Tragedy*, we might wonder why the Admiral's Men thought they had to revise it. The play had, after all, enjoyed great success during its last appearance at the Rose. Strange's Men's earliest recorded staging of their "Jeronymo" on 14 March 1592 brought in a sensational £3 11s., among the best takings anywhere in the "Diary," and the play continued to do very well over a twelve-performance run, with two more days of £3 revenues. When they brought it back during their short stint at the Rose in the winter of 1592/3, it again opened extremely successfully, yielding £3 8s. The Admiral's Men evidently felt no need to revise other old plays with established track records: they reintroduced *Doctor Faustus* without revisions in the autumn of 1594, for instance, and kept staging the play, unrevised, twenty-three more times even though it never showed the same commercial strength as *The Spanish Tragedy* did for Strange's Men, despite an equally powerful opening (£3 12s. on the first day, followed by a rapid decline into revenues just above £1). That, as Knutson has emphasized, was the point of having established old plays in your repertory: they did not require major investments, occasionally brought in a large nostalgic crowd, and generally delivered adequate takings. For the Admiral's Men to *introduce* as famous a play as *The Spanish Tragedy* into their repertory with instant revisions would seem to defeat the purpose. What is more, all the evidence the company had to go on would have told them that the play was perfectly commercially viable as it stood: it had a relatively recent history of great commercial strength at the Rose, it hadn't been seen on stage in years, and it had established itself as a popular commodity in the market for printed drama as well, with at least two editions since 1592. Why would a company waste resources on revising such a play?

The complications do not end there. If "Joronymo" was *The Spanish Tragedy* revised, the revisions must have been extraordinarily unwelcome because the play, after a strong opening, became one of the least successful shows in the Admiral's Men's records. Among the thirty-seven plays in their repertory that ran for at least ten performances, "Joronymo" ranked thirty-first. Its total income was similarly subpar, outranked by twenty-eight other titles. If this was an old play, the other revivals it resembled were "The Ranger's Comedy" and "The French Doctor" – not the revivals that *The Spanish Tragedy* might be expected to rival, such as *Doctor Faustus, Tamburlaine,* or *The Jew of Malta.* Those plays, none of which are "ne" in the "Diary," earned almost twice as much as "Joronymo." In fact, if one wanted to look for plays with similar earnings profiles in Henslowe's records, they are not difficult to find: new plays introduced in the 1596/7 season, such as "That Will Be Shall Be," or "A Woman Hard to Please," or "Vortigern," all have similarly low average revenues. "Joronymo" started significantly stronger than any of them, and ran out of steam almost instantly, with no recovery over the course of its subsequent eleven performances. All in all, it looks, commercially, like a new play that never took off. If that was the effect of introducing a revised *Spanish Tragedy*, we might wonder why the Admiral's Men did not simply revert to the original.

We might also wonder why instead, they paid an unprecedently large sum for more additions, not once, but twice, in 1601 and 1602, a mere four years later. If "Joronymo" was *The Spanish Tragedy*, it looks as though the company, mystifyingly, never tried to tap into the sense of familiarity that made other old plays in their repertory such reliable fallback options. Instead, they invested more and more money into revised versions of the old play. There is no parallel for such behaviour anywhere else in the "Diary." Explaining away Henslowe's "ne" makes "Joronymo" highly idiosyncratic. Alternatively, the case was utterly conventional: a play marked "ne" because when first performed, it had recently been commissioned and written. Either "Joronymo" is the most unusual entry in the *Diary*, or it is not unusual at all.

Yet many deeply learned scholars have been reluctant to accept that
Henslowe would use the same title for two different plays, especially if one
of them was as famous as *The Spanish Tragedy*. Section 2 will therefore mount
a broader argument, demonstrating that Henslowe appears in fact to have
recycled titles quite frequently and that clusters of plays about the same
subject, plotline, or character existed in the repertories of multiple companies
and that such plays were performed under identical, or near-identical titles.

2 Repertorial Clusters

Confronted with the overwhelming number of titles in Henslowe's records that
do not appear to refer to extant plays, scholars have frequently resorted to a
strategy John Astington has called "lumping": treating titles that can somehow
be connected to a surviving text as mere variants of the same, knowable entity.[58]
As Knutson has pointed out, the presuppositions that inform this practice,
particularly the "assumption that plays on the same general subject were the
same play, or revisions of the same play," skewed the foundational early
readings of Henslowe's records, obscuring especially "the commercial significance of duplicate plays, multi-part plays, and spin-offs."[59] Knutson's determi-
nation to counter this historical bias has produced a veritable cottage industry of
research on lost plays over the past decade. At the heart of this project lies the
invaluable Lost Plays Database; multiple monographs and collections of essays,
most recently David McInnis's *Shakespeare and Lost Plays*, have demonstrated
that it is possible to write about texts that no longer exist in rich and enlightening
detail.[60]

[58] John Astington, "Lumpers and Splitters," *Lost Plays in Shakespeare's England*,
ed. David McInnis and Matthew Steggle (Palgrave Macmillan, 2014), 55–71.

[59] Roslyn L. Knutson, *Playing Companies and Commerce in Shakespeare's Time*
(Cambridge University Press, 2001), 58.

[60] https://lostplays.folger.edu; McInnis and Steggle, eds., *Lost Plays in Shakespeare's
England*; Steggle, *Digital Humanities and the Lost Drama of Early Modern England*
(Ashgate, 2015); Roslyn Knutson, David McInnis, and Matthew Steggle, eds., *Loss
and the Literary Culture of Shakespeare's Time* (Springer/Palgrave Macmillan, 2020);

The "Lost Plays" project thrives on taking Henslowe and other historical sources at their word. For instance, W. W. Greg tried to argue that Henslowe's "Godfrey of Boulogne," a play in two parts, was in fact a single play identical to another title in the "Diary," "Jerusalem" – and that both of those titles stood for Thomas Heywood's *The Four Prentices of London*.[61] A more deferential reading of the "Diary" will acknowledge that the "Godfrey" play, unlike Heywood's, was a two-parter, and that "Jerusalem" is its own play, if thematically connected to the others on Greg's list. A somewhat trickier argument is involved in the strategy that forms the antagonist to Astington's "lumping": splitting. The splitters' approach expands one's sense of loss even beyond that effected by a literal reading of Henslowe. Astington, for example, cites the case of "William Longsword," a lost play by Philip Massinger, known only from a one-line reference in the records of Master of the Revels Henry Herbert. That 1639 drama was not the only play by that title: Henslowe noted a payment from the Admiral's Men to Michael Drayton for a "William Longsword" play in January 1599. Another document associated with Herbert lists three plays licensed in 1598 by Edmund Tilney, his Elizabethan predecessor. One of them, "allowed to be Acted the. 24 May. 1598," is "Sir William Longsword." Astington concludes that there may well have been at least three distinct early modern plays about this historical figure, two of them likely written and staged within twelve months of each other. All three texts hide behind essentially the same title, though. The scholar splitting that title into three different dramatic referents emulates, in a sense, early modern theatrical business practices: "commercial competition and emulation led to splitting, and differing dramatic versions of the same source material."[62]

McInnis, *Shakespeare and Lost Plays: Reimagining Drama in Early Modern England* (Cambridge University Press, 2021).

[61] See Knutson, *Playing Companies*, 58–9 and 159n19–20, discussing the arguments in Greg 2.166.

[62] Astington, "Lumpers," 92; see also Bawcutt 249. I would add that another of the three plays is "Richard Courdelyon;" Henslowe records multiple payments for "the funeral of Richard cordelion" in June 1598 (HD 90–2), which suggests that the date reported for Tilney's licenses is correct and that this "Longsword" is not the same play Drayton wrote for the company at the Rose playhouse.

That duplication was a commonplace "commercial strategy" among theatre companies is an insight central to repertory studies: companies hoped to exploit their own success through sequels, prequels, and spin-offs based on specific, often subsidiary, characters, but they also copied "the popular offerings of their competitors."[63] We already encountered a version of this strategy in Section 1: if the "Tamar Cham" plays in 1596 were actually "ne," Alleyn and the Admiral's Men commissioned plays drawing on material Alleyn appears to have enjoyed while with Strange's Men. As Martin Wiggins has pointed out in a discussion of the lost "Muly Molocco" play, it did not seem to matter that original and copy might have overlapped significantly in plot and structure. David Bradley believed that "Muly Molocco" in Henslowe's records must refer to *The Battle of Alcazar*, since "there could not have been another play about Abdelmelec [who was also known as Muly Molocco] based on the actual information available that was not exactly like this one."[64] But such overlap, writes Wiggins, is irrelevant: "the likelihood that two plays would have very similar narratives is not, in a competitive theatrical market, a *prima facie* case that there was only ever one such play" – as long as those plays belonged to separate repertories (BDC #918).[65]

This section is an exercise in what may seem like reckless splitting. Previous scholarly discussions of cross-repertory duplication have principally focussed on plays about historical figures, especially English kings. Henry V, Richard III, and Edward I all became the subjects of multiple plays performed by various companies, with scant differences in play titles.[66] I will argue here that copying, adapting, and repurposing material from other companies' plays also extended to more clearly fictional plots and characters, and that titles beyond those that take the form of a royal

---

[63] Knutson, *Repertory*, 71.

[64] David Bradley, *From Text to Performance on the Elizabethan Stage* (Cambridge University Press, 1992), 139.

[65] *The Battle of Alcazar* was published in 1594 with an attribution to the Admiral's Men; "Muly Molocco" is listed only as a Strange's Men play in Henslowe.

[66] See Knutson, *Playing Companies*, 61–2; Lukas Lammers, *Shakespearean Temporalities: History on the Early Modern Stage* (Routledge, 2018), 22–55.

name or *nom de guerre* may also require splitting. The case I am building here supports the hypothesis that Henslowe's "Je/oronymo" is not one, but two plays, and that further Hieronimo plays existed; I will outline that theory in Section 3. Here, I offer a more foundational claim: that neither the duplication of title nor the putative replication of narrative material in the case of *The Spanish Tragedy* was at all unusual, but that both were common practices in early modern theatre.

That playwrights read, saw, and copied texts and performances is hardly news. Typically, though, the relationship between a play – usually a play by Shakespeare – and other works has been a matter of source study. This has produced a tendency in theatre-historical and textual scholarship to construct diachronic relationships: one play succeeds another, in a company's repertory, or even in the theatrical marketplace. Shakespeare's *Hamlet* replaces the "Ur-Hamlet," which by 1594 is said to have belonged to the Lord Chamberlain's Men; his *Henry V* is understood as replacing, maybe displacing, the Queen's Men's *Famous Victories of Henry V*. In this mode of thinking, once a play becomes a source, it becomes unavailable as a viable theatrical offering. Emma Smith has recently lamented that traditional source study in general "tends to cancel the prior text and overwrite it retrospectively with the interest and presumed superiority of the later one," obscuring in the process that "Shakespeare's adaptations often coexist with the ongoing print life of these prior texts, in a relationship that is synchronous rather than teleological, intertextual rather than patrilinear."[67] I would extend this argument to *theatrical* coexistence: plays about near-identical subject matter, performed by different companies in different venues, shared overlapping audiences. Some of those plays were old, some were new, most were textually distinguishable to the attentive audience member. If anything, the conditions of the theatrical marketplace allowed for far more coexistence of closely related works than the market for printed books did.

What I propose here is that we should think of at least some titles or character names as representing repertorial clusters: plays from multiple

[67] Emma Smith, "Shakespeare As Adaptor," *The Arden Research Handbook of Shakespeare and Adaptation*, ed. Diana E. Henderson and Stephen O'Neill (Bloomsbury Arden Shakespeare, 2022), 25–37, 33, 31.

companies' repertories that shared identical plot elements, even dramaturgical structures, but not, beyond verbal borrowings and echoes, a textual form.[68] My point is not to hypothesize about lost duplicate plays in order to create more of the "blank[s] in textual history which the critic can inscribe as he pleases," to quote Emma Smith's astute critique of the scholarship on the "Ur-Hamlet," but rather to recover a theatre-historical context for plays that once formed part of such clusters and to bring back to scholarly attention an aspect of repertory practice that, when it has been addressed at all, has usually been dismissed as plagiarism or piracy.[69]

I will begin with an extended discussion of the various plays hiding in the shadow of Henslowe's short reference to "Friar Bacon," a title that appears ten times in the "Diary." These make for an illuminating case study because two of the plays survive, although one of them is much better known than the other. Unlike most of the scenarios I discussed earlier, arguing that "Friar Bacon" stands for a cluster of texts does not require positing that a now lost play once existed: it merely requires recognizing that the "Diary" references two separate extant plays. I will then briefly extend this argument to Henslowe's broader practice of using play titles, before finally developing an account of the importance of clusters of texts about the same characters or subjects as a feature of the early modern repertory – a feature that has been rendered functionally invisible by centuries of scholarly insistence on lumping.

The Friars Bacon

"Friar Bacon" first appears in Henslowe's records as an old play, the very first performance by Strange's Men entered in the "Diary," on 19 February 1592. They staged it just four times, exactly once a month, for the remainder of that season at the Rose, which ended when the Privy Council suspended all playacting following an apprentices' riot on June 23 (LSM 248). An outbreak

---

[68] Astington writes, in a similar context, of plays that make up the "Hamlet spectrum" ("Lumpers," 85).

[69] Emma Smith, "Ghost Writing: *Hamlet* and the Ur-Hamlet," *The Renaissance Text: Theory, Editing, Textuality*, ed. Andrew Murphy (Manchester University Press, 2000), 179–90, 179.

of the plague then kept the theatres closed until December. When Strange's Men returned, for what turned out to be a very short winter season curtailed by a resurgence of the plague at the end of January 1593, "Friar Bacon" came back with them, now on a more rapidly paced schedule: they put it on three times between January 10 and 30. On none of these occasions did the play yield particularly impressive revenues. For its first appearance, Henslowe recorded a mere 17s. 3d. of takings, less than half the average for that season. And during the brief second season, the only play earning less on average was another old piece, "Mandeville." There is every indication that this "Friar Bacon" was already little more than a dependable fallback option in the company's repertoire by 1592, and its commercial utility was fading fast.

London would not see a company patronized by Lord Strange again, but a "Friar Bacon" reappears in Henslowe's lists shortly after the Rose was allowed to reopen on 1 April 1594. At that point, however, the title is associated with "the Quenes men & my lord of Susexe to geather" – and again, it is the opening performance (HD 21). Precisely what Henslowe meant when he described two companies as appearing "together" has long been debated by theatre historians, but in this instance at least, the two troupes probably did not collaborate but rather took turns.[70] If so, the Queen's Men offered just two plays, both of which were later printed with title pages advertising a connection to this company. One of these was their "Friar Bacon," and although revenues fell somewhat short of those earned by Sussex's Men, this Bacon play averaged almost twice what Strange's identically named piece had earned.

For decades, theatre historians assumed that only one "Friar Bacon" existed. Greg asserted that all the entries referred to Robert Greene's *Friar Bacon and Friar Bungay*, but since Greene's play advertised itself as "plaid by her Maiesties seruants" when published later in 1594, and since it was certainly not a new work, Greg needed to construct a rather convoluted account.[71] Originally, he argued, the script belonged to the Queen's Men, from whom it

---

[70] See Helen Ostovich, Holger Schott Syme, and Andrew Griffin, "Locating the Queen's Men: An Introduction," in *Locating the Queen's Men, 1583–1603: Material Practices and Conditions of Playing* (Ashgate, 2009), 1–23, 6–8.

[71] The play was entered in the Stationers' Register on 14 May 1594, a month after its last recorded performance at the Rose (BDC #822).

passed, via Alleyn, to Henslowe, who became the new owner and lent it, first, to Strange's Men and then *back* to the Queen's Men.[72] As Scott McMillin noted fifty years ago, that narrative should quickly have been revised after the publication, in 1936, of a second "Friar Bacon" play that survives only in a manuscript in the Duke of Northumberland's library at Alnwick Castle.[73] Unhelpfully, this play is now known by the title its twentieth-century editor, William Lindsay Renwick, invented: *John of Bordeaux*. The text itself gives no title at all; T. Duffus Hardy, Deputy Keeper of the Record Office, thought in 1870 that the manuscript should be catalogued "as a drama without a title but probably originally entitled 'Friar Bacon' as he seems to be the principal character in the play." "Friar Bacon" is also the title printed on the spine of the volume in which the play was bound, together with another dramatic manuscript, shortly thereafter.[74]

Renwick thought the play could also be called "The Second Part of Friar Bacon." In one sense, this would have been a more helpful choice than *John of Bordeaux*, signalling the text's place in the repertory cluster of "Bacon" plays. In another sense, though, the "second part" designation is counterproductive since it implies a similar relationship as that between the first and second parts of *Tamburlaine* or of *Henry IV*, or of the many "serial" plays in the Admiral's Men's repertory. Knutson has noted that such seriality did not necessarily demand narrative continuity (her key example being *2 Robin Hood*), although it did imply a relationship between plays in the same

---

[72] Greg 2.149, 2.162. There is no evidence that Alleyn was a member of the Queen's Men.

[73] Scott McMillin, "The Ownership of *The Jew of Malta*, *Friar Bacon*, and *The Ranger's Comedy*," *English Language Notes* 9 (1972): 249–52, 250. See also Scott McMillin and Sally-Beth MacLean, *The Queen's Men and Their Plays* (Cambridge University Press, 1998), 90.

[74] Quoted in William Lindsay Renwick, ed., *John of Bordeaux or The Second part of Friar Bacon* (Malone Society Reprints, 1936), v. For the most recent account of that manuscript, see James Purkiss, "*John of Bordeaux*: Performance and the Revision of Early Modern Dramatic Manuscripts," in *Early British Drama in Manuscript*, ed. Tamara Atkin and Laura Estill (Brepols, 2019), 123–36. Since referring to this play by its modern title undercuts the very argument I am pursuing, I avoid the use of "*John of Bordeaux*" here.

company's repertory.[75] Often, both plays would also be written by the same author(s). But to the best of my knowledge, no company advertised plays in their repertory as the second halves of plays found in other troupes' offerings.

That the Alnwick manuscript represents a text written *after* Greene's *Friar Bacon and Friar Bungay* is evident, as previous scholars have noted.[76] It occasionally alludes to events in that play, and three of its characters – Bacon, his rival Vandermast, and the German Emperor – play prominent roles in Greene's play. Although the rivalry between Bacon and Vandermast carries through from *Bacon and Bungay*, the structural similarity of the two plays, with their central tragicomic romance plots, makes them appear more like two separate treatments of a near-identical scenario. Darren Freebury-Jones's recent close analysis of the text makes it appear unlikely that Greene wrote both plays, as had often been surmised. What stands out in that analysis are the dramaturgical differences between *Bacon and Bungay* and the Alnwick text: the two plays stage similar subject matter, but in different tones, attitudes, and even theatrical registers, with the Alnwick text lacking "Greene's sophisticated treatments" of "visual theatre" as well as his "multi-layered staging."[77] In a similar vein, Manley and MacLean have noted the displacement of Greene's "bluff patriotism" in favour of "quasi-religious sentiment" (LSM 94). In other words, the Alnwick play reads less like a "second part" than like the outcome of a process that might have begun with a company other than the Queen's Men commissioning a playwright to produce their own version of a "Friar Bacon" – a play that ticks many of the same theatrical boxes as *Bacon and Bungay*, also revolves around a romance plot, and also features spectacular

---

[75] Knutson, *Repertory*, 50–3.

[76] See, for example, Bronwyn Johnston, "Who the Devil Is in Charge? Mastery and the Faustian Pact on the Early Modern Stage," in *Magical Transformations on the Early Modern English Stage*, ed. Lisa Hopkins and Helen Ostovich (Ashgate, 2014), 31–46, 44; and Laurie Maguire, "John Holland and *John of Bordeaux*," *Notes and Queries* 231 (1986), 327–33.

[77] Darren Freebury-Jones, *Reading Robert Greene: Recovering Shakespeare's Rival* (Routledge, 2022), 92–101, 100.

magic fights with Vandermast, but changes the setting and takes a significantly different dramaturgical approach. The later play is not so much a sequel to or an adaptation of Greene's script, nor necessarily a "rival"[78] to it, but can perhaps be best thought of more neutrally as an alternative take, a different company's own "Bacon" play, less a phenomenon of fierce competition than a repertory item comfortably coexisting with other versions of itself in the theatrical marketplace.

That this company was Strange's Men is made probable not just by the appearance of a "Friar Bacon" play in Henslowe's records, but also by marginal references in the manuscript to the actor John Holland. Holland's name only appears in documents connected with the Chamberlain's Men: he is cast in multiple roles in the backstage plot for the lost "Second Part of the Seven Deadly Sins," and is mentioned as one of Jack Cade's followers in *2 Henry VI* (first printed in 1623). Before David Kathman definitively dated the "Seven Deadly Sins" document to 1597–8, it was long considered a prime piece of evidence for the membership of Strange's Men.[79] It has now lost that function, but Holland's appearance in the plot and in the Alnwick manuscript nonetheless links that version of "Friar Bacon" to Lord Strange's players. Most of the founding sharers in the Chamberlain's Men came from Strange's company, and in many ways the Chamberlain's Men can be seen as its successor organization. The Alnwick playscript in fact shows further ties to the Chamberlain's Men: it was annotated for performance by a playhouse scribe whose distinctive hand also produced several other important documents connected to the company at the Shoreditch Theatre. That scribe is Hand C, the bookkeeper who edited the revised version of *The Book of Sir Thomas More*, wrote the "Seven Deadly Sins" plot, and was probably the Chamberlain's Men's principal scribe until sometime around 1602, when he seems to have moved to the Admiral's Men at the Fortune playhouse.[80]

---

[78] McMillin, "Ownership," 250.

[79] David Kathman, "Reconsidering *The Seven Deadly Sins*," *Early Theatre* 7 (2004): 13–44.

[80] Hand C's career largely remains a blank in theatre-historical scholarship; my brief account here is based on a paper I delivered at the Shakespeare Association of America in March 2016 ("The Perigrinations of Hand C").

The Alnwick manuscript thus not only provides us with solid grounds for positing that the "Friar Bacon" entries in Henslowe's "Diary" refer to multiple plays rather than a single text (or a single work with multiple revisions); it also contains evidence, in the form of Hand C's annotations, that one "Friar Bacon" moved from the Rose to the Theatre, the Chamberlain's Men's first home. Despite its somewhat lackluster performance in Strange's Men's repertory, it may have continued to function as dependable filler in the repertory staged at the Theatre.[81] This longer institutional history then makes it unlikely that the final reference to a "Friar Bacon" in the "Diary" has anything to do with the Alnwick manuscript. That reference appears in the form of a payment to Thomas Middleton on 14 December 1602 "for a prologe & A epeloge for the playe of bacon for the corte" (HD 207). No "playe of bacon" is mentioned in Henslowe's records for more than eight years before this entry, but since they are hardly complete it is certainly possible that the Admiral's Men commissioned their own Bacon play after November 1597, when Henslowe stopped keeping a tally of which titles were performed when. If so, the Bacon cluster may have consisted of three distinct plays by 1602. Alternatively, it is possible that the Admiral's Men acquired the right to perform the Queen's Men's *Bacon and Bungay*. When that play was reprinted decades later, in 1630, its title page advertised it as "lately plaid by the Prince *Palatine* his Seruants." That company, the Palsgrave's Men, were the Admiral's Men, two patrons later; but by 1630 they barely existed anymore, having collapsed after a catastrophic two-year plague that lasted from 1625 to 1627. Drawing inferences about the Admiral's Men's repertory from the Palsgrave's stock of plays is complicated by the fact that all their playbooks were destroyed when the Fortune playhouse burned down in 1621. *Friar Bacon and Friar Bungay* may only have entered the Palsgrave's repertory when they were trying to rebuild after that catastrophe: it was old, available in print, and may not have been played by anyone in decades, the Queen's Men having disappeared at the end of Elizabeth I's reign. In other

---

[81] Manley and MacLean likewise argue that the Alnwick play was Strange's Men's "Friar Bacon" and that it subsequently moved to the Chamberlain's Men; see LSM 93–6.

words, that *Bacon and Bungay* was performed at the rebuilt Fortune after 1622 – assuming "lately" does not refer to events a decade or more ago – tells us almost nothing about a "Play of Bacon" performed by the Admiral's Men at court in the winter of 1602.[82] Then again, there is a connection between the Queen's Men and the Elizabethan Admiral's Men: John Singer, the great comic actor, moved from the Queen's company to the Admiral's by late 1594. It may be that he owned *Friar Bacon and Friar Bungay* and brought it to the Rose when he joined them (although in that case, the play went unperformed for at least three years). That there is no evidence of its presence in their repertory before 1602 cannot count as evidence of its absence: Henslowe's records are simply too incomplete and, after 1597, are particularly silent on standard repertory planning decisions such as the revival of old plays without revision or the need for new costumes. To sum up, then: there was a small cluster of "Friar Bacon" plays from the 1590s which we can trace in the repertory of at least two companies, and there may have been a third such play belonging to yet another troupe. Henslowe's "Diary," however, appears to refer to two, perhaps even three, of those plays by the same name (with minor variations).

Obscured Multitudes

"Friar Bacon" is by no means the only title in Henslowe's "Diary" that can be suspected of polyreferentiality. Both sets of "Tamar Cham" entries and the two "French Comedies," as I discussed in Section 1, may fall into the same category. In a similar vein, David McInnis has argued against conflating the entries for a "Fortunatus" in early 1595, which are for the revival of an old play, with those recording payments to Thomas Dekker for *Old Fortunatus* in November 1599, basing his edition of the latter play instead on the assumption that "the Fortunatus legend was popular with early modern playgoers," sustaining both a revival of an older play on the subject in 1595 and the "acquisition of a new play on the topic (Dekker's) introduced in late 1599."[83]

---

[82] See EPT 546; see also BDC #822.

[83] David McInnis, "Introduction," in *Old Fortunatus*, Revels Plays (Manchester University Press, 2020), 6.

In another case, the slipperiness of Henslowe's titles is self-evident. Strange's Men and the Admiral's Men owned a "Knack" play each: *A Knack to Know a Knave* and *A Knack to Know an Honest Man*. Henslowe records both titles as "the Knacke" far more frequently than under their full (distinguishable) names. *A Knack to Know a Knave* is listed as "the knacke" or "the cnacke" for four out of its seven performances in 1593–4. The Admiral's Men's *Knack to Know an Honest Man*, identified by versions of its full title three times in the fall of 1594, becomes "the Knacke" thereafter – except after two breaks in its performance schedule, when Henslowe again gives the full title. It is thus merely "the Knacke" on fourteen out of twenty occasions. When the play was revived after its longest hiatus of seven months, in November 1596, Henslowe entered it simply (and ambiguously) as "the cnacke to knowe."[84] Or rather, not ambiguously at all: the Admiral's Men only had the one "Knacke" play, and contextually, the reference would not have been confusing to anyone at the Rose in 1596.

Henslowe, we need to remind ourselves, did not keep his records for posterity. As long as a shorthand title was sufficient for him, and perhaps for the company, to understand what was meant by it, he probably would not have worried about continuities or ambiguities of reference. He and the Admiral's Men knew, after all, that they only had one "Knack" play in their stock. Likewise, Strange's Men would not have been confused about which "Friar Bacon" play they owned. Henslowe also made no effort whatsoever to distinguish titles of plays performed at the Rose from similarly named plays staged elsewhere. To give just a few examples: we have a Henslowe "Henry V" that is clearly not Shakespeare's, and probably not the Queen's Men's *Famous Victories of Henry V* either; we have a "Longshanks" that is probably not Peele's *Edward I*; a "Jerusalem" that may or may not be one of the several surviving plays with "Jerusalem" in the title; a "Four Plays in One" staged by Strange's Men that probably has nothing to do with the

---

[84] HD 19–20, 25–8, 30–1, 34, 36, 54. It is worth noting here the imprecision of Henslowe's entries, which vary from "a Knacke to Know a noneste" to "the Knacke to Knowe & oneste man" and "the Knacke to Know a nonest man;" he correctly records the play title's indefinite article only once. I will return to this in my discussion of the *Shrew* plays.

"Five Plays in One" performed by the Admiral's Men; and a "Comedy of Humours" that could refer to at least three different "Humours" comedies on stage somewhere in the late 1590s (even though it almost certainly is Chapman's *Humorous Day's Mirth*).[85]

This cavalier attitude to play titles was not specific to Henslowe. Even the Master of the Revels, it seems, was not especially concerned about what the plays he read were called. When George Buc inscribed his license onto the final page of a new Middleton tragedy he had just allowed in October 1611, he laconically described it as "this second Maydens tragedy (for it hath no name inscribed)" – a title Greg thought was "inappropriate," since all it did was signal that the play superficially had something in common with Beaumont and Fletcher's recent *Maid's Tragedy*. For Buc, however, a title saying little more than "a play that reminds me of another play" was evidently good enough.[86]

Glimpsing Clusters: Henslowe and Beyond

Henslowe's two best-known ambiguous references come from the same group of performances, by "my Lord Admeralle men & my Lorde chamberlen men" (notably not "to geather"), at the playhouse in Newington Butts in June 1594 (HD 21). Here, we find a "hamlet" (not "ne," on 9 June) and "the tamynge of A shrowe" (likewise not "ne," on 11 June). Typically, these have been read as merely sounding like plays by Shakespeare. The "Hamlet" in question has been identified as an earlier play about the Danish prince, the *Ur-Hamlet* that has haunted the scholarly imagination since the nineteenth century.[87] The "Shrew," by way of insisting on a literal reading of Henslowe's entry, has been confidently linked to the *Taming of a Shrew*

[85] HD 33–4, 36–7, 47–8, 323; HD 30–6, 47–8, 317, 323; HD 17; HD 16 and 57–60; HD 58–60, 323.

[86] See Dutton, *Mastering the Revels*, 215–16; Greg, *Dramatic Documents*, 227.

[87] See Zachary Lesser, *Hamlet after Q1: An Uncanny History of the Shakespearean Text* (University of Pennsylvania Press, 2015), 6–8 and 172–95; and on Ur-texts more broadly, Roslyn L. Knutson, "Ur-Plays and Other Exercises in Making Stuff Up," in *Lost Plays*, ed. McInnis and Steggle, 31–54.

entered in the Stationers' Register on 2 May 1594, and printed sometime thereafter with a title page advertising its performance by "the *Right honorable the Earle of* Pembrook his seruants."[88] In both cases, then, scholarly orthodoxy splits Henslowe's titles off from surviving Shakespeare plays. However, the multiplication of referentiality is immediately contained by a narrative of succession. The *Ur-Hamlet* soon became, and was displaced by, Shakespeare's *Hamlet* – as E. K. Chambers put it, "the old play is not likely to have survived Shakespeare's" – even as *A Shrew*, imagined as a Chamberlain's Men's property, in James Marino's words, "grew more complicated and poetically accomplished through revision" as it turned into *The Shrew*.[89] In these accounts, the plays behind Henslowe's entries precede Shakespeare's versions and are subsequently succeeded by them. They do not coexist.

That Henslowe's "hamlet" did not belong to the Admiral's Men is plausible enough since the play never appears in any of their detailed performance records. Even if we assume, though, that all the plays performed at the Newington playhouse can definitively be assigned to either the Admiral's Men or the Chamberlain's players after June 1594 (an assumption I would resist), Henslowe's records do not in fact permit the assertive identifications the received accounts rely on.[90] *Shrew* is perhaps the more obvious case in point: recall the many entries for the two *Knack* plays alone, in which the "Diary" gets the indefinite article in both plays' titles right exactly *once* in twenty-seven records. That example alone demonstrates that any faith

---

[88] Stephen Roy Miller, ed., *The Taming of a Shrew: The 1594 Quarto*. New Cambridge Shakespeare: The Early Quartos (Cambridge University Press, 1998), 31. I myself have previously insisted on the importance of Henslowe's "A," as has, for instance, James Marino, in *Owning William Shakespeare: The King's Men and Their Intellectual Property* (University of Pennsylvania Press, 2011), 49.

[89] E. K. Chambers, *William Shakespeare: A Study of Facts and Problems* (Clarendon, 1930), 2 vols., 1:411; Marino, *Owning*, 49.

[90] One of the plays in question would be *Titus Andronicus*, and I have argued elsewhere that this play remained with Pembroke's Men until at least 1596; a similar trajectory can be posited for the Newington "Hamlet." See "Three's Company" and Section 4.

in Henslowe's accurate recording of this kind of detail, which to him must have been irrelevant, is surely misplaced. However, if the "Diary" entry cannot be clearly linked to *A Shrew* at all and might as easily refer to the play ultimately published in 1623 as Shakespeare's *The Shrew*, the succession narrative I have sketched loses its key data point. Similarly, although the existence of a play about Hamlet written before the treatment printed in the second quarto of 1604/5 is beyond doubt, it is not at all clear that the "hamlet" in the "Diary" is the same as that tragedy – which is not to say that we must identify it with one of Shakespeare's *Hamlet*s either.

To briefly rehearse the evidence: in 1589, Thomas Nashe contributed a preface to Greene's *Menaphon* in which he referred to writers (more specifically, "translators"), who, reading "English *Seneca*" "by candle light" concoct "whole *Hamlets*" of "tragical speaches."[91] Who exactly Nashe's target is has long been disputed; I am persuaded by Lukas Erne's restatement of the argument that many of the specific allusions and jibes in the passage fit Thomas Kyd.[92] In any case, though, by 1589, a tragedy about Hamlet and influenced by Senecan rhetoric appears to have existed. A second famous reference to such a play occurs in Thomas Lodge's 1596 *Wit's Miserie*, which recalls "the Visard of ye ghost which cried so miserably at ye Theator, like an oister wife, Hamlet, revenge."[93] If Lodge has a relatively recent performance in mind, that "Hamlet" must have been staged by the Chamberlain's Men, the only company we can locate at the Theatre in Shoreditch between 1594 and 1596. In that case, it seems highly likely that Lodge's "Hamlet," with its miserable ghost, is the same play recorded in Henslowe's "Diary" in June 1594 – if *that* "Hamlet" moved to Shoreditch with the Chamberlain's Men. Most contemporary scholars doubt that Shakespeare's *Hamlet* could have been written as early as that, in any of its three versions; generations of critics have also insisted on a verbatim reading of Lodge, noting that Shakespeare's ghost never cries "Hamlet, revenge."[94] Therefore, the "Hamlet" in Henslowe

---

[91] Quoted in Lukas Erne, *Beyond* The Spanish Tragedy: *A Study of the Works of Thomas Kyd* (Manchester University Press, 2001), 147.

[92] Ibid., 147–50. [93] Quoted in Chambers, *Shakespeare*, 1:411.

[94] For a recent dissenting opinion, see Terri Bourus, *Young Shakespeare's Young Hamlet* (Palgrave Macmillan, 2014), especially 144–79, who argues that Q1 of

and in Lodge must either be a very early (lost?) first attempt by Shakespeare, or another play about the Danish prince. Was it the same play Nashe satirized, though? Erne thinks so, writing matter-of-factly that "one of the few things we know about Kyd's *Hamlet* is that, contrary to Belleforest's novella [the putative source text], it featured a ghost" – because Lodge tells us about a ghost in a "Hamlet" play.[95] We do not in fact know that these were the same plays. "Hamlet, revenge," the Ghost's apparent catchphrase, appears not only in Lodge, but also in Thomas Dekker's *Satiromastix*, a play about which I will have much more to say in Section 4. In *Satiromastix*, written and registered in 1601, the phrase is associated with "Paris Garden" – that is, the Swan playhouse, a venue with no documented connection to the Chamberlain's Men.[96] Finally, Chambers notes, in the same sentence in which he asserts that the emergence of Shakespeare's *Hamlet* surely drove the "old play" from the theatrical marketplace, that "Hamlet, revenge" remained a recognizable tag as late as Samuel Rowlands's pamphlet *The Night-Raven* in 1620.[97]

The *Ur-Hamlet* narrative, which imagines a linear progression from one play (Kyd's) to Shakespeare's, cannot easily accommodate all these allusions. Neither is it clear who invented the ghost, nor if all theatrical "Hamlet"s were ghost plays. The "Hamlet, revenge" phrase seems to have featured in more than one theatrical treatment of the story since it was spoken *both* at the

---

Hamlet represents a very early play of Shakespeare's, and that all references to "Hamlet" plays, from 1589 to 1620, are to one of the extant printed versions. A very early date for the text printed in Q1 has been supported by Gary Taylor in "Shakespeare's Early Gothic *Hamlet*," *Critical Survey* 31 (2019): 4–25. I find the theory that Q1 of *Hamlet* represents Shakespeare's earliest treatment of the material credible but see no need to accept the late 1580s dating nor to insist on Shakespeare's play(s) as the singular referent of all allusions.

[95] Erne, *Beyond*, 150.

[96] Thomas Dekker, *Satiromastix*, in *The Dramatic Works of Thomas Dekker*, ed. Fredson Bowers (Cambridge University Press, 1953), vol. 1, 299–396, 4:1.121–2 (all further references cited parenthetically). Bourus, in a reading I don't find wholly persuasive, disputes this association (*Young Hamlet*, 252n42), interpreting the line instead as drawing a contrast between the Swan and the Globe.

[97] Chambers, *Shakespeare*, 1:411.

Theatre and at the Swan. If we hold with the centuries-old scholarly consensus that "Hamlet, revenge" is the tag that distinguishes lost "Hamlet" play(s) from Shakespeare's *Hamlet*(s), we are then almost forced to conclude that there probably were at least two such plays in circulation in London around the time Shakespeare wrote his own.[98]

The lines of transmission between all these dramatic Danes are blurry, though: the *Hamlet* versions we know may or may not derive from Kyd's. The Chamberlain's Men may have owned the play Nashe mocked in 1589 five years later, to be replaced after a few years with Shakespeare's reworking of the material. Or the "hamlet" they staged at Newington Butts in 1594 may have been a different adaptation, with a ghost so notorious for his oyster-wifely loudness by 1596 that the enduringly popular subject matter demanded a new dramatic treatment. Or perhaps Kyd's version ended up with Pembroke's Men at the Swan, possibly after passing through Newington Butts in 1594 – in which case Erne is right after all that Kyd invented the ghost and therefore invented the catchphrase too. In *that* case, the different adaptation in the Chamberlain's Men's repertory derived its ghost and his catchphrase from Kyd even though they did not own his version; Shakespeare may have written the Q1 version to replace the script that became Pembroke's. And so on: the fragmentary evidence allows for a proliferation of possible narratives, anything from one "Hamlet" play (Shakespeare's, revised twice) to three (Kyd's tragedy, which was either the one in Henslowe and at the Theatre or the one at the Swan; whichever of the two wasn't Kyd's play; Shakespeare's) to a possible seven or so (Kyd's play; the play in Henslowe; the play at the Theatre; the play at the Swan; Shakespeare's *three* versions). I don't think the full roll call makes for a persuasive narrative, but neither does the traditional assumption that there can

---

[98] Janet Clare has cautioned, though, that the phrase might have been invested with too much evidentiary power: "perhaps the remark is a conflated recollection, combining salient moments of the play … rather than a faithful record of a particular theatrical moment" (*Shakespeare's Stage Traffic: Imitation, Borrowing and Competition in Renaissance Theatre* (Cambridge University Press, 2014), 169); see also Bourus, *Young Hamlet*, 146. Given that the phrase is used independently by three different writers, it seems more plausible to me to treat it as a verbatim quotation from a now lost Hamlet play.

only have been one *Ur-Hamlet* before Shakespeare's took over the field. To me at least, the most comprehensive reading of the fragments suggests that there was more than one pre-Shakespearean tragedy about Hamlet and that various Hamlet versions continued to exist in a variety of repertories long after 1601.

That such coexistence of closely related plays in multiple companies' repertories was not unusual might be more apparent if the Stationers' Company had followed practices similar to the informal agreements that seem to have governed the relationships between acting troupes. However, the regulation of the print trade created a climate inimical to the publication of, say, multiple "Hamlet" plays by competing stationers. As Peter Blayney noted more than two decades ago, the owner of a registered title "had not only the exclusive right to reprint the text, but also the right to a fair chance to recover his costs. He could therefore seek the [Stationers'] Company's protection if *any* book – not necessarily a reprint or plagiarism of his own copy – threatened his ability to dispose of unsold copies of an existing edition."[99] There is no evidence that similar restrictions existed in the theatre.[100] What clearly crossed a line – and would have brought players

---

[99] Peter Blayney, "The Publication of Playbooks," *New History of Early English Drama*, ed. Cox and Kastan, 383–422, 399. English history plays provide the most visible instance of the Stationers' Company's conventions producing a market for printed drama that differed greatly from the theatrical marketplace reflected in the London-based troupes' repertories. Whereas multiple plays about the same historical figures coexisted in the playhouses, typically, only one or two of those plays reached print, producing an impression, from the perspective of book history, of the English history play as a stagnant and fading genre (see my "'But, what euer you do, Buy': *Richard II* As Popular Commodity," *Richard II: New Critical Essays*, ed. Jeremy Lopez (Routledge, 2012), 223–44, 228–9).

[100] Beyond the question of regulations, the two markets also called for different strategies: stationers and playing companies made different commercial decisions. As Amy Lidster has recently argued regarding historical drama, there was a "disjunction between stage and page patterns"; the apparent dominance of Shakespeare's plays "is more precisely ... a print development" and not "representative of repertory patterns in the theatre" (*Publishing the History Play in the Time of Shakespeare: Stationers Shaping a Genre* (Cambridge University Press, 2022), 87).

into conflict with the Master of the Revels – was for one company to simply start performing another company's play, whether printed or not. (The theft of a "Jeronimo" play by a boys' company alluded to in *The Malcontent*, as discussed in the Introduction, is the only evident case of this nature.) On the other hand, commissioning a new version of an existing play, however closely it may follow the original, a freshly written script approved by the Master of the Revels before its first performance, was not just acceptable, but standard practice. Some *playwrights*, especially those with a keen eye on the book market, objected to other writers doing such work. Thus Robert Greene seems to accuse the author of the Strange's Men's *Fair Em* of plagiarism, and Ben Jonson liked to wield the same rhetorical cudgel.[101] Acting companies, and most playwrights, had no such qualms. Lucy Munro and Sarah Wall-Randell have hypothesized that companies maintained collections of books as source texts for new plays; the letters from Robert Daborne to Henslowe cited by Munro can certainly be read this way. However, I would also want to entertain the notion that when Daborne asked Henslowe to "send me the Book y[o]u promysd" or to "let me have p[er]vsall of any other book of y[our]s," the books he meant were playbooks, printed or in manuscript, performed by the Henslowe-hosted Lady Elizabeth's Men or not.[102]

Rather than taking the word of uncommonly possessive dramatists or the regulations of the Stationers' Company as normative, we need to understand the writing of plays as primarily a theatrical practice. As such, plays had venues and performers. They might have had recognizable plots

---

[101] See Freebury-Jones, *Robert Greene*, 94–5. On Jonson, see, for example, Joseph Loewenstein, *Ben Jonson and Possessive Authorship* (Cambridge University Press, 2002), 94–9; and Colin Burrow, *Imitating Authors: Plato to Futurity* (Oxford University Press, 2019), 234–78.

[102] Lucy Munro, "Writing a Play with Robert Daborne," *Rethinking Theatrical Documents*, ed. Stern, 17–32, 19; Wall-Randell, "What Is a Staged Book? Books As 'Actors' in the Early Modern English Theatre," ibid., 128–51, 132–3. Letters from Daborne to Henslowe, 5 November and 3 May 1613, in W. W. Greg, ed., *Henslowe Papers: Being Documents Supplementary to Henslowe's Diary* (A. H. Bullen, 1907), 77, 69. Munro notes that the "books" Daborne mentions may include "other source materials, such as older playbooks" (19).

and characters, but only rarely did they, in the theatre, have authors.[103] It may be true, then, that the Alnwick "Friar Bacon" owes much to Greene's *Bacon and Bungay*, but in the theatre, that was probably all but irrelevant – because audiences would have encountered the former as *Strange's Men's* "Bacon" play, embodied by actors they could only have experienced in the context of that performance; whereas they would have seen the latter as the *Queen's Men's* "Bacon" play (after 1594, if they were well-read, perhaps as Robert Greene's "Bacon" play performed by the Queen's Men), embodied differently by a different set of actors. By the same token, it is unnecessary to posit that the Chamberlain's Men owned Kyd's "Hamlet": they had one play in the "Hamlet" cluster, and then, once Shakespeare wrote his, they had another. Their ownership of one of those older plays, however, was not a necessary precondition for Shakespeare's writing of his *Hamlet*. They may even have kept more than one Hamlet play in their repertory. After all, the company was not averse to staging multiple scripts drawing on the same subject matter, as their ownership of two *Richard II* plays shows.[104]

Which text had launched a cluster – that is, the question of origins – may not have been especially interesting, or even legible, to early modern audiences.[105] Making connections between performances of similar material by different companies (or even the same company) surely was one of the pleasures of the frequent playgoer. Comments such as John Manningham's famous description of a 1602 performance of *Twelfth Night* at the Middle Temple as "much like the comedy of errores, or Menechmi in Plautus, but most like and neere to that in Italian called Inganni" imply no disappointment

---

[103] Compare Clare's observation that "the circulation of different plays with similar themes and materials was part of early modern theatrical culture, and these plays were identified first with companies, and slowly, but not consistently, with authors" (*Stage Traffic*, 12).

[104] For the non-Shakespearean *Richard II* Simon Forman saw at the Globe in 1611, see Chambers, *Shakespeare*, 2:339–40.

[105] See Eoin Price, "Early Modern Drama Out of Order: Chronology, Originality, and Audience Expectations," *Playing and Playgoing in Early Modern England: Actor, Audience and Performance*, ed. Simon Smith and Emma Whipday (Cambridge University Press, 2022), 161–80.

or disapproval when they highlight similarities. For Manningham, these similarities provide a foil for noteworthy differences such as the "good practice" of the gulling of Malvolio.[106] From that perspective, reportorial clusters should be less surprising to us than popular plays not being replicated in the repertories of other companies. Why, we might ask, did the Admiral's Men seemingly *not* have a tragedy about Hamlet? Or is that what is hiding behind their suggestively titled "Osric" (HD 56)?

A Cluster of Shrews

Seen through the logic of a repertory of thematic clusters, the existence of two Elizabethan *Shrew* plays appears neither perplexing nor a problem: the only thing remarkable about these two texts is that both survived. *A Shrew* and *The Shrew* constitute prima facie evidence that multiple plays with practically identical titles and shared plot elements and character names, but with notably different structures and totally different texts (on a line-by-line basis), coexisted in the theatrical market.

Thinking of *A Shrew* as Shakespeare's source or as a corrupt version of *The Shrew* are the two models that have dominated scholarly discussions for the past century, certainly since Peter Alexander declared the 1594 printing a "bad quarto" produced via memorial reconstruction.[107] Barbara Hodgdon outlined an alternative approach in her Arden Third Series edition, characterizing the two plays "as representing different stages of an ongoing theatrical 'commodity' that was formed at some point in the early 1590s and has been undergoing mutations ever since."[108] Eschewing conventional certainty about chronologies, she instead concludes that "*A Shrew* and *The Shrew* obviously know one another, a knowledge most pronounced in plot features" (395). Hodgdon's position expressly owes a debt to Leah Marcus's important reading of the *Shrews* as "a cluster or network of related texts that can be fruitfully read together and against each other as

---

[106] See Chambers, *Shakespeare*, 2:327–8.

[107] Peter Alexander, "*The Taming of A Shrew*," *Times Literary Supplement*, 16 September 1926: 614.

[108] *The Taming of the Shrew*, ed. Hodgdon, Arden Shakespeare Third Series (Methuen, 2010), 36.

'Shakespeare.'"[109] These formulations share common ground with my own model of repertorial clusters, but the continued critical insistence on "Shakespeare" as the rubric under which this "theatrical commodity" or "network of related texts" can be most fruitfully interpreted remains a limitation. Even when *A Shrew* is taken seriously as a play, it is read as "a critique of values operating in the received text," not as an equal node in the network of Shrew texts.[110]

My purpose here is not to offer an alternative reading of *The Taming of a Shrew*, but simply to realign the balance between the two plays. The very idea that something is wrong with *A Shrew* is a direct consequence of its association with *The Shrew* in Shakespeare scholarship. Early modern readers do not seem to have considered the play printed in 1594 notably flawed. On the contrary: *A Shrew* was quickly reprinted in 1596 and saw a third edition in 1607. Few other Elizabethan comedies were reissued even once, and this kind of lasting print success for a comedy has almost no parallels (others, particularly Jonson's *Every Man Out of His Humour*, Jonson, Chapman, and Marston's *Eastward Ho*, and Marston's *The Malcontent* also were reprinted three times, but in very quick succession; *A Shrew* is seriously bested only by *Mucedorus*). Sir John Harington's reference to "the booke of taming a shrew" in his 1596 *Metamorphoses of Ajax* implies that the printed play, as a work of literature, was familiar material.[111] The reception history of *The Shrew* is murky, but *A Shrew* was a popular play, certainly in print and presumably on stage as well. Many modern editors of Shakespeare's play may find this success bewildering given the "clearly inferior" quality of the play, its "incompetent versification," "execrable" verse, "slackness in diction," and "feeble repetition of words."[112] We should at least recognize, though, that these deplorable weaknesses did not

---

[109] Leah Marcus, *Unediting the Renaissance: Shakespeare, Marlowe, Milton* (Routledge, 1996), 124.

[110] Ibid., 116. For a critique, see Clare, *Stage Traffic*, 87–99.

[111] Quoted in Hodgdon, *Shrew*, 11.

[112] H. J. Oliver in his Oxford Shakespeare edition of *Taming of the Shrew*, quoted in Graham Holderness and Bryan Loughrey, "Introduction," *A Pleasant Conceited Historie, Called The Taming of a Shrew*, Shakespearean Originals: First Editions (Routledge, 2014), 13–36, 14.

trouble early modern readers, just as the absence of such weaknesses was not enough to sell more than a single print-run of, say, *Much Ado About Nothing*.

Placing *A Shrew* within a Shakespearean sphere not only does the play no favours, it also misrepresents how it was received, and likely how it was written. It inevitably reduces *A Shrew* to what Alan Galey has cannily called "an object of Shakespearean interest."[113] At the same time, the anonymous author of *A Shrew* appears to suffer so much by direct juxtaposition with Shakespeare that even the title of "author" becomes unjustifiable: one of the play's modern editors, Stephen Roy Miller, insists on calling the playwright a "compiler" to highlight "the use of borrowed material" in the text.[114] By that standard, as we have seen, Robert Daborne was often little more than a mere compiler too, and the same could probably be said for many working playwrights of the period at least some of the time.

If we approach *A Shrew* instead as a play that knew – or was known by – *The Shrew*, part of a larger set of shrew-taming plays to which Fletcher's *The Tamer Tamed* also belongs, we might be able to see it as a highly representative piece of theatrical writing.[115] Large parts of it may well be derivative, but hardly "memorially reconstructed": it follows the structure of some of the scenes in *The Shrew* but makes no attempt to reproduce Shakespeare's verse. On the other hand, the text deliberately quotes passages from Marlowe's plays, especially *Tamburlaine* and *Doctor Faustus*, to which *A Shrew* owes no dramaturgical debts.[116] The author here is doing exactly what we would expect an early modern playwright to do – and what Shakespeare does in many of his plays (and may, in fact, have done in *The*

---

[113] Alan Galey, "Signal to Noise: Designing a Digital Edition of *The Taming of a Shrew*," *College Literature* 36 (2009): 40–66, 56.

[114] Miller, *A Shrew*, 4.

[115] For a recent reading of all three plays and the context of early modern shrew narratives, see Erin E. Kelly, "Shakespeare's New Shrew," The Taming of the Shrew: *The State of Play*, ed. Heather C. Easterling and Jennifer Flaherty (Bloomsbury Arden Shakespeare, 2021), 19–35.

[116] See Marcus, *Unediting*, 121, for a shrewd reading of the dramaturgical function of these "stage quotations of tragedies well known to audiences in the early 1590s."

Shrew).[117] It matters little for my argument here which of the two plays came first: however they came into being, they eventually coexisted in the same theatrical environment. Early modern audiences, like Manningham, may have registered parallels and differences between the two texts, but most would probably not have placed them in a hierarchy of original and copy – or if they did, may have noted that *both* plays adapt elements of George Gascoigne's *Supposes*. Perhaps they noticed what Miller points out in his edition: *A Shrew* often is a more straightforward play than *The Shrew*. Shakespeare tends to complicate his sources, *A Shrew* tends to simplify them.[118] Again, these features do not map onto a structure of original and copy. Adaptations can simplify and cut down; they can also elaborate and extend. Audience members at a performance of *The Shrew* who had read *A Shrew* may well have recognized the connections and might have seen the Chamberlain's Men's play as an elaboration of the play they knew. Most likely, though, playgoers who saw *A Shrew* at the Swan and *The Shrew* in Shoreditch within a few months of each other would merely have thought of the one as "the book of the Taming of a Shrew the players have at Paris Garden," and of the other as "the book of the Taming of a Shrew the players have at the Theatre." "Shakespeare" probably would not have been a relevant category of reception for them.

* * *

Let me end with one more brief illustration of the normalcy of duplication across repertories – in this instance, immediate duplication – which shows that clustering remained theatrical practice into the 1620s. In September 1624, Sir Henry Herbert licensed *two* plays about the real-life murder of Joan Tindall, seemingly on the same day. The one he allowed first, by Dekker, Ford, Rowley, and Webster, to be performed at the Red Bull, was given a day's head start. The other, by Thomas Drue, was, as far as Herbert was concerned, "the same Trag[edy]," even though it was obviously a

---

[117] Emma Smith regards "adaptation as intrinsic to Shakespeare's poetry and dramaturgy: to the texture of his writing as well as the construction of his plays" ("Shakespeare As Adaptor," 26).

[118] See, for example, Miller, *A Shrew*, 9–11, 15–17.

different text, by a different playwright, submitted by a different company. To Herbert's mind, there was nothing objectionable, problematic, or, as far as we can tell, especially noteworthy about any of this.[119]

Here is the case I hope to have made in this section: that Henslowe commonly used identical or near-identical titles for distinct plays, and that, in the broader theatrical marketplace, plays on the same subject, character, or familiar storyline were clustered under near-identical titles as well. The coexistence of such plays across repertories was unlikely to be replicated in the highly selective printed record of early modern drama because the Stationers' Company placed a premium on titles and treated a similarity of titles as a commercial threat. In the theatrical marketplace, by contrast, similarity of titles and plots was always countered by self-evident differences in company identity and venue.

At this point, let me now at last return to *The Spanish Tragedy* – and Henslowe's perhaps newly unfamiliar "Joronymo."

3 The Hieronimo Complex

Bringing together the attributionist argument linking Shakespeare to the revised *Spanish Tragedy* with my own interpretation of Henslowe's recording habits and the existence of repertorial clusters, let me now, over the next three sections, offer two related revisionist narratives: that "Jeronimo" stood not for a single play, but for a cluster of scripts, mostly but not exclusively tragedies, in the repertories of at least four companies; and that *The Spanish Tragedy*, after 1594, belonged to the Chamberlain's/King's Men.

The Admiral's Men without The Spanish Tragedy

As I noted in the Introduction, theatre historians have been unable to ignore that Richard Burbage played Hieronimo, so some sort of connection between the company in which he was a sharer for most of his career and Kyd's play has long been acknowledged. Knutson went further than most when she argued more than twenty-five years ago that the Chamberlain's/

---

[119] Bawcutt 154; see also Dutton, *Mastering the Revels*, 300.

King's Men had a Hieronimo play of their own, but even she remained undecided as to the identity of that play. She contemplated the possibility that it may have been *The Spanish Tragedy*, but also wondered whether "it was merely a clone of it in the sense that the many plays about King Henry V duplicated one another." What Knutson – along with virtually all her colleagues – never seriously questioned was the assumption that the Admiral's Men staged Kyd's tragedy: they "acquired the text owned formerly by Strange's men, perhaps thanks to Alleyn and his instinct for good theatrical property." As an almost necessary consequence of that view, she argued that the Admiral's players "revived it in 1596–7, probably with revisions, and probably again in 1601–2, with more revisions (Jonson's)."[120]

However, the new evidence does not quite support such a timeline. The longest of the revisions, the "Painter's part," must have been written before 1601: Marston parodies the scene in *Antonio and Mellida*, a play entered in the Stationers' Register on 24 October 1601 and performed between early 1599 and then.[121] The additions thus predate the work for which Jonson was paid. If Shakespeare was one of the revising contributors, *The Spanish Tragedy* must already have been in the repertory at the Globe before Jonson revised the Admiral's Men's "Joronymo" – unless we assume that Shakespeare worked for a rival company on the side. There is no reason to believe he would have acted against his own company's commercial interests in such a fashion.[122] That the *Parnassus* play associates Burbage with the role of Hieronimo by late 1601 cements the case against Jonson being paid to alter *The Spanish Tragedy* in 1602. It seems we are forced to conclude

---

[120] Knutson, *Repertory*, 91–3.

[121] See Taylor and Loughnane, "Canon and Chronology," 530, and Vickers, "Shakespeare's Additions," 15–16.

[122] Taylor and Loughnane seem to envisage Shakespeare writing for the Admiral's Men when they write, in discussing possible dates for the additions, "it is not inconceivable that the 1597 performances included the additions, but we think a later date is more likely" ("Canon and Chronology," 530). I argue that, on the contrary, those 1597 performances have no bearing on the dating of Shakespeare's new material.

either that the Admiral's Men had Kyd's play but lost it before *Antonio and Mellida* was written, or that they never owned it at all. Since we know of no movements of actors from the Rose company to the Chamberlain's Men in those years, the latter strikes me as the far more likely scenario. It is also the one best supported by Henslowe's "Diary."

Brian Vickers has offered a third, unfortunately implausible, scenario to explain Shakespeare's contributions. He proposes that *both* companies staged Kyd's play at the same time:

> Since *The Spanish Tragedy* had been played in London from
> about 1587 to 1588, and published in 1592 with no declaration
> on its title-page associating it with a theatre company, then,
> according to Elizabethan pragmatic practices neither Strange's
> nor the Admiral's Men could claim it as their exclusive prop-
> erty, and other companies were free to perform it.[123]

There is no evidence whatsoever that such "pragmatic practices" existed. Neither is there a basis for assuming that the information given on the title pages of printed playbooks affected the privileges and rights of acting companies vis-à-vis the plays in their stock. If there were, we might wonder why the Admiral's Men did not revive the anonymous *Knack to Know a Knave*, staged very successfully by Strange's Men at the Rose and published in 1594 "as it hath sundrie tymes bene played by ED. ALLEN and his Companie."[124] Since "ED. ALLEN" had rejoined the Admiral's Men in 1594, that title page surely would have given them at least as much right to this popular comedy as any other group of actors had – if the actions and choices of stationers had any impact on how theatre companies conducted their business. Nothing we know indicates that this was the case.

What is more, as Richard Dutton has pointed out, the Master of the Revels would not have licensed the same text for two companies, and it is unlikely that either of the troupes in question, with their privileged standing

---

[123] Vickers, "Additions," 16.

[124] *A Most Pleasant and Merie New Comedie, Intituled, A Knacke to Knowe a Knaue* (London: Richard Jones, 1594), sig. A1r.

at court, would have performed a play without Tilney's permission (Dutton 116). Herbert's later records show that he would not let a company perform an old play that had previously belonged to another troupe without the permission of the previous owner, and he probably followed long-established practice in this regard.[125] "Performing rights," affirms Dutton, "were specific and exclusive" (Dutton 166).

However we approach the "Joronymo" question, then, it seems overwhelmingly likely that the "specific and exclusive" license the Admiral's Men acquired in January 1597, as the "ne" tag probably confirms, was for their own Hieronimo script. Perhaps its curious commercial trajectory, discussed in Section 1, reflects that very combination of familiarity and novelty: the exceptionally successful opening performance (bested, as we saw, only by the second "ne" opening of "Alexander and Lodowick" that season) may indicate that expectations were high for a new take on the Hieronimo material. The precipitous drop-off after the second performance indicates that those expectations were not fulfilled. Word may have spread that whatever the Admiral's Men were staging, it was not the Hieronimo play the crowd thought they were going to get.

Hieronimo after Kyd

The late 1590s was the time when *The Spanish Tragedy* as written by Kyd turned into a textual relic of a theatrical event no longer available in its original form, replaced by not just a revised text but a cluster of versions and adaptations. We get a glimpse of this transition in the "Praeludium" to Jonson's *Cynthia's Revels*, performed by the Children of the Chapel in late 1600, with its satirical portrayal of an audience member who wants a lost original back, "swear[ing] down all that sit about him, 'that the old *Hieronimo*', as it was first acted, 'was the only, best, and judiciously penned play of Europe.'"[126] By then, at least two "new" Hieronimoes had been

---

[125] See, for example, Bawcutt 144.

[126] *Cynthia's Revels*, ed. Eric Rasmussen and Matthew Steggle, in *The Cambridge Edition of the Works of Ben Jonson*, gen. eds. David Bevington, Martin Butler, and Ian Donaldson, 7 vols. (Cambridge University Press, 2012) (subsequently cited as CWBJ), Praeludium 165–7. Performed in late 1600,

staged, the version to which Shakespeare contributed and the Admiral's Men's "Joronymo." *The Spanish Tragedy* itself, in the theatre, had become an object of nostalgia. Thinking back to my earlier discussion of the Shrew plays, though, we might also note that the kind of audience member who pays undue attention to hierarchies of original and copy and dwells on plays as they were, is here, as elsewhere in Jonson, a figure of ridicule. Jonson presumably did not know that he would be contributing to *two* repertorial clusters within a year of writing *Cynthia's Revels*, with his clearly large-scale revision of "Joronymo" at the Fortune as well as the "Richard Crookback" play he wrote at the same time. His satire is not a preemptive act of authorial self-defense, but it recognizes a basic fact of early modern playwriting.

The clustering of "Hieronimo" plays began earlier, though. By 1592, some of Strange's Men's performances of their "Jeronymo" were already preceded by what Knutson describes as its "forepiece," "The Spanish Comedy" – or, as Henslowe renders it, "spanes comodye donne oracioe."[127] As I will argue in Section 5, this comedic prequel, apparently about Hieronimo's son Horatio, likely transferred to the Chamberlain's Men's repertory together with *The Spanish Tragedy*. There may also have been a second Hieronimo tragedy by 1592, as the printing history of *The Spanish Tragedy* suggests. The first extant quarto advertises itself on its title page as "Newly corrected and amended of such grosse faults as passed in the first impression," and by December 1592 its publisher, Edward White, was locked in a legal battle with his fellow stationer Abel Jeffes over the rights to the book.[128] It is at least conceivable that Jeffes, who had registered his rights in the play on 6 October 1592, owned a *different* text, which he may have printed first (although no copies survive); and that the extant quarto, printed in violation of the Stationers' Company's regulations, represents White's

Cynthia's Revels was entered in the Stationers' Register on 23 May 1601 (see CWBJ 1.431).

[127] Knutson, "Repertory," 470; HD 16–19. The title varies a fair amount, morphing, by May 1592, into "the comodey of Jeronymo" (HD 18).

[128] For a detailed account of the dispute, see John Henry Jones, *The English Faust Book: A Critical Edition Based on the Text of 1592* (Cambridge University Press, 1994), 47–50. See also Knutson, *Repertory*, 92.

attempt to get the version of the text in his possession into print no matter what. The case, which led to both White and Jeffes being fined by the Company, is murky, but the two stationers apparently came to an agreement: the second quarto, issued two years later, reproduces White's text, and was still published by him – but this time, he paid Jeffes to print the volume. This resolution seems to correspond precisely to the arrangement Blayney describes for disputes where two different plays with near-identical titles were owned by rival stationers. With two different Hieronimo texts possibly in circulation already, the conflict between Jeffes and White appears to anticipate the similar, if preempted, dispute between Thomas Creede as the owner of *The Famous Victories of Henry the Fifth* and Thomas Millington and John Busby, the owners of Shakespeare's *Henry V*. In that slightly later case, Creede's text disappeared from the market, but he had the printing of both quartos of Shakespeare's play.[129]

Another alternative Hieronimo play – or perhaps the version Jeffes owned, if that is what happened – was probably performed by Pembroke's Men at the Swan before July 1597, with Ben Jonson as Hieronimo. That case is so intriguing that I will discuss it in detail in Section 4; here, I will simply offer it as one more possible member of the cluster. Finally, there are Jonson's revisions. Henslowe records two payments to him for "additions": first, on 25 September 1601, 40s., a sum at the upper end of charges for revisions and additions elsewhere in the "Diary"; then, on 22 June 1602, a second payment of £10 "in earneste of A Boocke called Richard crockbacke & for new adicyons for Jeronymo" (HD 182 and 203). The normal payment for a new script was £6, precisely what the Admiral's Men appear to have paid Jonson, over the course of nine months, for rewrites of their "Joronymo." Given the poor commercial performance of the 1597 play, these payments suggest two things to me. First, the Admiral's company continued to think that they needed a Hieronimo tragedy in their repertory: the cluster remained culturally significant enough in late 1601 that they needed to maintain a stake in it. Second, they first asked Jonson to fix the existing version, but then, in a second step, commissioned him to produce a complete rewrite – presumably because the initial additions were insufficient to turn the previously unimpressive "Joronymo" into a popular success. Given that he was paid a fee equivalent to that for a new play, we should probably think of the end product of this process as Jonson's own full-length adaptation of the Hieronimo material.

Exactly what any of those other plays may have brought to Kyd's plot, how they may have varied characters and story, is almost completely beyond reconstruction. We can catch intriguing glimpses, however, in contemporary allusions to Hieronimo plays, which appear in at least sixty-six texts.[130] Forty-eight of them apparently refer to *The Spanish Tragedy*, often with verbatim quotations, but the rest are either ambiguous or reference events not contained in Kyd's text or the additions. The minority of allusions are thus reminiscent of those that underpin the "Ur-Hamlet" narrative. For instance, Dekker, in *The Seven Deadly Sins of London* (1606), has "the Ghost in *Jeronimo*" rising up crying "Revenge" – which the ghost does not do in *The Spanish Tragedy*. That Dekker knew Kyd's play well is indisputable; he quotes a line from it in the very pamphlet in which he also seems to misrepresent the events of the play.[131] Unless he is not misrepresenting *The Spanish Tragedy* at all, but rather alluding, as his contemporaries would have understood, to two separate treatments of the Hieronimo material. In one of those versions, a vindictive ghost rose from the stage trapdoor. Shackerley Marmion seems to reference just such a scene decades later, in *Holland's Leaguer* (1632), when he writes of "Jeronimoes sonnes ghost in the Garden" crying "Murder, Murder." Emma Smith may be right that Marmion "confuse[s] separate incidents" in *The Spanish Tragedy*, but equally plausibly, he may recall a *different* play, in which Horatio's ghost rose to demand that his father avenge his murder.[132]

It is tempting to see in this hint of a different plot element a possible connection between the Hieronimo cluster and the Hamlet spectrum. The scene was clearly memorable, given that Marmion recalled it in the 1630s; it may have featured in the first or second "Joronymo" or in the version Jonson acted with Pembroke's Men – or all three. I am tempted to imagine it

---

[130] Emma Smith lists fifty-nine references in "Hieronimo's Afterlives," in *Thomas Kyd: The Spanish Tragedie*, ed. Smith, Renaissance Dramatists (Penguin, 1998), 133–59. I have independently identified seven further allusions.

[131] Ibid., 139, 146. [132] Ibid., 139.

as a novelty introduced in Jonson's rewritten "Joronymo" in 1601/2. Shakespeare was working on *Hamlet* around the same time. Encountering in this rival Hieronimo play the ghost of a murdered son who urged his father to avenge his death may have inspired him to answer with a revenge tragedy adopting the theatrical device while reversing the generational dynamics.

The Hieronimo Effect

By the late 1590s, "Jeronimo" no longer referred to a single play, let alone a clearly identifiable tragedy by Thomas Kyd. It stood for a complex of texts performed variously by Strange's Men, the Chamberlain's Men, Pembroke's Men, the Admiral's Men, the Children of the Chapel, and the King's Men, in at least six separate venues. What marks the pervasive cultural influence of *The Spanish Tragedy* is precisely that it spawned such a large number of theatrical versions: it was not merely a popular play, but a cultural phenomenon.[133] Trying to determine precisely when a reference gestures towards the original and when it alludes to a derivative version is not only counterproductive, since privileging Kyd's play isolates it artificially from its own influence; it is also often impossible – and that impossibility itself illustrates how pervasive the Hieronimo effect was.

This slipperiness of reference is best illustrated with an example. On a piece of scrap paper from the Revels' Office dating from between 1615 and 1621, "The Tradgedy of Jeronimo" is listed alongside other recognizable titles: Beaumont and Fletcher's *Philaster* and *The Maid's Tragedy*, Middleton's *Hengist, King of Kent*, and a "Hamlet" that may or may not be Shakespeare's. E. K. Chambers argued that this document was part of the planning process for the Christmas season at court: the plays named are those George Buc was considering for performance. Helpfully, the list is numbered, seemingly offering multiple options for each day:

---

[133] This generative influence was not limited to England. In Germany and Holland, up to seven versions were written and staged. See Erne, *Beyond*, 127–34; and Willi Flemming, ed., *Jeronimo, Marschalck in Hispanien: Das deutsche Wandertruppen-Manuskript der* Spanish Tragedy (Olms, 1973).

[1?] [Th]e Maior of Quinborough
        or Hengist K. of Kent
[T]he Scholler turnd to schoole
        againe
[2] The Falce Frend
The Maides Tragedy
3 The Cambridge Playe of
        Albumazar and Trinculo
The Tradgedy of Ham[let]
The Tradgedy of Jeronimo
4 The History of Phil[aster]
        or Love lies a bleed[ing]
The Comedy of
The T
    of[134]

Each number appears to be linked to two plays: the manuscript is badly
deteriorated, and a "5" has probably disappeared to the left of the final two
lines. The only outlier is day three, with the (amateur) production from
Cambridge considered in addition to one of two professional shows. If that
is the logic of the list, it seems to give a known King's Men play for each day
of the festivities. We cannot know, though, if any day includes a choice of
two offerings from that company, or if the two options are always a
performance by the King's Men and one by another troupe. The only day
with two plays we can identify with extant texts is the third, and here both
the Hieronimo cluster and the Hamlet spectrum trip us up. Accepting that
the King's Players owned *The Spanish Tragedy* does not help because the
document does not identify *which* Hieronimo play it means.

---

[134] Frank Marcham, ed., *The King's Office of the Revels 1610–1622* (Marcham, 1925),
       10–11. See also E. K. Chambers, "Review of Marcham, The King's Office of the
       Revels, 1610–1622," *Review of English Studies* 1 (1925): 479–84; and Gary
       Taylor and John Lavagnino, eds., *Thomas Middleton and Early Modern
       Textual Culture: A Companion to the Collected Works* (Oxford University
       Press, 2007), 332–3, 410–12.

Buc evidently saw no need to remove the ambiguity himself, although he annotated the list and added alternative titles for two of the plays. He knew and cared to write down that *The Mayor of Quinborough* was also known as *Hengist, King of Kent* and that *Philaster* also went by *Love Lies A-Bleeding*, but he did not think to note that "The Tradgedy of Jeronimo" was famous as *The Spanish Tragedy* too. Or, alternatively, perhaps *this* "Jeronimo" was *only* known by that title. Complicating matters further, although the King's Men dominated the court calendar in those years, the "Joronymo" company (now the Palsgrave's Men) were summoned for a single performance on 3 January 1619, which happens to be the most likely year for Buc's list.[135]

Whose "Tradgedy of Jeronimo," then, was being considered for court performance? The King's Men's ancient classic, recently reprinted with a new title-page illustration and a new surtitle ("Hieronimo is mad againe")?[136] Or a play owned by the Palsgrave's Men, written in 1597, rewritten by Jonson in 1601–2, and still in their repertory at the Fortune two decades later? That Buc did not amend the title written by his clerk, together with the presence of the Palsgrave's Men in the court calendar in 1619, makes the latter, to me, more likely. Saying more would be claiming too much, but certainty was not, after all, the point of this example. Slipperiness was. And the "Tradgedy of Jeronimo" is a prime instance of that: a single title irreducibly standing for multiple plays and performance histories.

Even after the theatres were officially shut down in 1642, the recognition that "Jeronimo" represented a cluster of plays lingered. Three booksellers' catalogues published in the 1650s, purporting to list "all such Plays that ever were Printed," mention more than one Hieronimo play.[137] The first of these booklists, published by Richard Rogers and William Ley in 1656, includes "Hieronimo both parts," but not *The Spanish Tragedy*, and does not give an

---

[135] John Astington, *English Court Theatre, 1558–1642* (Cambridge University Press, 1999), 252. No play titles are recorded for those years.

[136] *The Spanish Tragedie: OR, Hieronimo is mad againe* (London: William White for John White and Thomas Langley, 1615).

[137] On these catalogues, see Adam G. Hooks, "Booksellers' Catalogues and the Classification of Printed Drama in Seventeenth-Century England," *Papers of the Bibliographical Society of America* 102 (2008): 445–64.

author's name (then again, *Hamlet* is listed without an author as well). The second, considerably more elaborate catalogue was issued by Edward Archer later that same year. It includes "Hieronimo, both parts," ascribed to "*Will. Shakespeare*" and identified as "H[istories]" *and* a "Spanish Tragedie," by "*Tho. Kyte*" and marked as a "T[ragedy]."[138] Five years later, when Francis Kirkman assembled a third "true, perfect, and exact Catalogue" of "printed and published" plays, *The Spanish Tragedy* had disappeared again and "Hieronimo" had been disaggregated into "Hieronimo 2. part" and "Hieronymo 1st. part" – both "T[ragedies]," both anonymous.

As far as we know, Archer's list is incorrect and only two Hieronimo plays ever reached print. His confusion might be informed by an abiding memory that there *were* more than those two, that there was a distinction between *The Spanish Tragedy* and a different version of Hieronimo, and that Shakespeare had something to do with at least one of those plays. Kirkman removes the uncertainty about authorship by simply deleting Kyd's and Shakespeare's names. Arguably, his approach distorts matters more than Archer's. It certainly had the curious consequence of leaving Kirkman's catalogue without an entry for *The Spanish Tragedy* – the name that appeared on the title pages of ten quartos, and thus had a more pervasive presence in the market for printed books than any play other than *Mucedorus*. Kirkman's choices also remind us of what that print history obscures: that in the theatre, Hieronimo had left *The Spanish Tragedy* behind.

4 Ben Jonson's Hieronimo

Thomas Dekker's claim that Ben Jonson once played Hieronimo is perhaps the most intriguing anecdote in the performance history of the Hieronimo cluster. My arguments in the preceding sections should encourage us to take such anecdotes seriously as glimpses of theatre-historical misconstruals. Reading Dekker's jokes in *Satiromastix* as evidence of things we have

---

[138] All three catalogues quoted from W. W. Greg, *A Bibliography of the English Printed Drama to the Restoration* (Bibliographical Society/Oxford University Press, 1939–59), 3 vols., 3:1321, 1324, 1333, 1336.

ignored or forgotten reveals new perspectives both on the extent and reach of the Hieronimo phenomenon, and, more surprisingly, on Jonson's career as a professional player. Jonson, as has already become apparent in Section 3 and as will be obvious in Section 5, has more connections with *The Spanish Tragedy* and its adaptations than any other early modern playwright. The evidence I present here shows that the origins of this lifelong engagement were theatrical as well as intertextual: Jonson participated in the Hieronimo complex as an actor before he helped shape it as a writer.

In *Satiromastix*, two references to Jonson's acting serve to remind Horace, Dekker's caricature of Jonson, of his past as a player. First, Tucca (Dekker's mouthpiece) snipes that he has "seene thy shoulders lapt in a Plaiers old cast Cloake, like a Slie knaue as thou art: and when thou ranst mad for the death of Horatio: thou borrowedst a gowne of *Roscius* the Stager, (that honest Nicodemus) and sentst it home lowsie, didst not?" (1.2.354–8) Later, he expands the association when he demands of Horace, "thou hast been at Parris garden hast not?" prompting the latter's admission "I ha plaide Zulziman there." Finally, Tucca paints the now actor-scorning Horace as once keen to act on stage:

> thou putst vp a Supplication to be a poore Iorneyman
> Player, and hadst beene still so, but that thou couldst not
> set a good face vpon't: thou hast forgot how thou amblest (in
> leather pilch) by a play-wagon, in the high way, and took'st
> mad Ieronimoes part, to get seruice among the Mimickes.
> (4.1.121–32)

Horace's supposedly haphazard career was ended when "the Stagerites banisht thee into the Ile of Dogs" (132–3).

As everywhere in *Satiromastix*, the allusions come thick and fast, and many of them seem impossible to unpack (for instance, "Roscius" might be Alleyn or Burbage, but why is either of them an "honest Nicodemus"?). If Dekker is making fun of Jonson's actorly past, though, the joke surely only works if the basic facts are right: Horace/Jonson really did act at "Paris Garden"; he played a Hieronimo who ran "mad for the death of Horatio"; he also (or only?) performed that role on tour; his costume for the role was borrowed from another player, presumably from another company; and he played the role of "Zulziman," or another role in a play with that title.

In 1601, "Paris Garden" meant the Swan, which had opened in 1595. The list of possible first occupants of the new venue is relatively short.[139] Perhaps the most plausible candidate is Pembroke's Men, who acted there when the playhouses were shut down in July 1597, shortly before two of their sharers (Robert Shaa and Gabriel Spencer) were arrested for the staging of a "very seditious and slanderous" play – along with someone who "was not only an actor but a maker of part of the said play": Ben Jonson.[140] That play was "The Isle of Dogs," cowritten with Thomas Nashe, and the evident referent of Dekker's allusion to a career-ending banishment. The performance effectively eliminated Pembroke's Men as a London company. Like most troupes, they also toured the country, as records from 1595 and 1596 show. In other words, much of Tucca's portrayal of Horace's theatrical career fits with the hypothesis that Jonson acted with Pembroke's company in the mid-1590s.

"Zulziman" might be Thomas Kyd's *Soliman and Perseda*. Erne argues that Pembroke's Men may have performed the play at court in the 1592/3 Christmas season.[141] The company owned major Elizabethan works of drama, including *Edward II*, *The First Part of the Contention of the Two Famous Houses of York and Lancaster*, and *The True Tragedy of Richard Duke of York*, *Titus Andronicus*, and *The Taming of a Shrew*. It would not be surprising to find Kyd's play in their repertory. Alternatively, the reference may be to another play featuring Suleiman the Magnificent, part of a thematic cluster that also included Henry Chettle's lost 1598 "Vayvode."[142] However, if Dekker means that Jonson played the titular

---

[139] See William Ingram, *A London Life in the Brazen Age: Francis Langley, 1548–1602* (Harvard University Press, 1978), 153–66.

[140] EPT 102. See also Ingram, *London Life*, 167–96, and Misha Teramura, "Richard Topcliffe's Informant: New Light on *The Isle of Dogs*," *Review of English Studies* 68 (2017): 44–59.

[141] Erne, *Beyond*, 163.

[142] See Misha Teramura, "The Admiral's *Vayvode* of 1598," *Early Theatre* 18 (2015): 79–99; and https://lostplays.folger.edu/Vayvode.

male lead in *Soliman and Perseda*, such a claim is difficult to square with the assertion that he was a "poor Iorneyman Player." Hired hands are not recorded as playing such major roles in the period. Similarly, the idea that a mere "jobbing actor"[143] would play Hieronimo in *The Spanish Tragedy*, one of the more dominant roles in the early modern repertoire, whether on tour or in London, is hard to reconcile with what we think we know about how acting companies functioned.

Might Jonson have been a sharer in Pembroke's Men? Might Dekker's portrayal of him as a poor performer, dependent on borrowed robes and merely filling in for others while on tour, be a deliberate distortion? We have at least some evidence that he may have been a sharer. For one, there is a puzzling entry in Henslowe's "Diary," dated 28 July 1597 and seemingly the first in a projected list of payments: "R[eceive]d of Bengemenes Johnsones Sharre" (HD 52). Its meaning is obscure, but Henslowe also records a loan of £4 he gave to "Bengemen Johnson player" (HD 238) the very same day (as well as an earlier loan of five shillings, granted on 5 January 1597). More than a century ago, Alwin Thaler pointed out that similar arrangements can be found elsewhere in the "Diary." For instance, Gabriel Spencer, who had joined the Admiral's Men after the collapse of Pembroke's company, borrowed more than £2 from Henslowe and repaid his debts in instalments drawn from "his share in the gallereyes" (HD 67) – that is, the portion of the revenues he could claim as a sharer in the Admiral's company.[144] But while Spencer was a member of the Admiral's company, Jonson was not: at his arrest in August 1597, he is definitively identified as an actor with Pembroke's Men. The playhouses were shut down on 28 July 1597, the very date of Jonson's first repayment to Henslowe, and he cannot have been a sharer in the Admiral's Men then. He may, however, have had that status with Pembroke's Men – and, as Chambers suggested in response to Thaler, the arrangement may have been for Henslowe to receive payments directly from the share of revenues due to Jonson from the Pembroke's Men's landlord at the Swan, Francis

---

[143] Ian Donaldson, *Ben Jonson: A Life* (Oxford University Press, 2011), 103.

[144] Thaler, "Bengemenes Johnsones Share," *Modern Language Review* 16 (1921): 61–5, 64.

Langley.[145] Given that neither the company nor Jonson had any revenues after 28 July, the fact that the list ends with its first entry supports Chambers's hypothesis. As far as I know, nobody has rethought the matter in the century since.[146]

Jonson's second trace as a sharer is, strictly speaking, an absence. After Shaa, Spencer, and Jonson were released from custody in early October 1597, Shaa and Spencer reunited with three other sharers from Pembroke's Men who had in the intervening months joined the Admiral's Men: William Bird (alias Borne), Thomas Downton, and Richard Jones. All five men, however, were still under contract with Langley to perform at the Swan and had signed a bond for a £100 penalty should they play elsewhere in London. Langley now threatened to sue those five actors – but not "the three of the company" who did not make the move to the Admiral's Men (EPT 444). *Those* three are never named in the suit. One of them may very well have been Ben Jonson.

The legal arguments between the five players and Langley illustrate the significant professional standing of Pembroke's Men. The defendants describe themselves as experienced actors who "have of long time used and professed the art of stage-playing" (EPT 442). Langley evidently considered them a suitable company for his splendidly decorated new playhouse, a sufficiently desirable group of performers to warrant a non-compete bond, and already successful enough to be good for the threatened penalty. That they were no mere gang of ragtag hirelings is further demonstrated by their careers after the five defendants joined the Admiral's Men: Shaa immediately took on a leadership role in the management of his new company; Bird is a perennial presence in the "Diary"; and Spencer, although he only had a year to live before Jonson killed him in a duel in September 1598, left such a strong impression that Thomas

---

[145] Quoted in W. W. Greg, "Bengemenes Johnsones Share," *Modern Language Review* 16 (1921): 323.

[146] Jakub Boguszak briefly considers the possibility that Jonson may have been a sharer but prefers to think of him as the mere journeyman player of Dekker's satire; see *The Self-Centred Art: Ben Jonson's Parts in Performance* (Routledge, 2021), 53.

Heywood would still praise "his deserts" as late as 1612.[147] Downton and Jones had been leading members of the Admiral's Men when the company began playing at the Rose in 1594 and were persuaded to join Pembroke's Men at some point between then and 1596 – a move they presumably considered no worse than lateral. In other words, the "Mimickes" with whom Jonson kept company were one of the major troupes of their day, operating at the same level of expertise as the Admiral's and Chamberlain's Men in London's theatrical ecosphere. Jonson's role with them may have resembled Shakespeare's with the Chamberlain's since he was both a player and an in-house playwright. "The Isle of Dogs" was not his first contribution. His earliest extant play, *The Case is Altered*, was almost certainly premiered by Pembroke's Men, and, given that Francis Meres in 1598 could describe Jonson as among "the best for Tragedie," he probably established that reputation via their repertory as well.[148]

If Jonson, then, was a core member of Pembroke's Men rather than just a hired hand, perhaps he did play Soliman. Tucca's lines may contain another, less obvious allusion to one of his roles. Long ago, Fredson Bowers proposed that Dekker's slightly odd reference to Horace once wearing an "old cast Cloake" "like a Slie knaue as thou art" implies that Jonson played Sly in *The Taming of the Shrew*. But since Bowers could not conceive of the two *Shrew* plays as coexisting in two rival repertoires, he took the indefinite article in Henslowe's one reference to a *Shrew* play literally and insisted that *A Shrew* belonged to the Chamberlain's Men as of June 1594. Consequently, he had to argue that Jonson played Sly when he was an actor in *the Chamberlain's company* after 1597, a hypothesis that, in the absence of any documentary support, rightly never caught on.[149] An alternative reading of

[147] HD 363 (indexing Shaa's fifty-eight business transaction); HD 348 (seventeen transactions for Bird); Edwin Nungezer, *A Dictionary of Actors* (Yale University Press, 1929), 337.

[148] *The Case Is Altered*, ed. Robert Miola (CWBJ), dates the play to "the first half of 1597" (1.3); Meres, *Palladis tamia Wits treasury* (London: Peter Short for Cuthbert Burby, 1598), sig. Oo2r.

[149] Fredson Bowers, "Ben Jonson the Actor," *Studies in Philology* 34 (1937): 392–406, 400–1.

the evidence is sustainable, though, especially in light of my arguments in Section 2: that *A Shrew* remained the property of Pembroke's Men; that Jonson played the role of Sly during his tenure with the company, from sometime in 1595/6 to the summer of 1597; and that, for this role, he may have worn, not inappropriately, an old, cast-off cloak. If this seems a reasonable interpretation, a set of possible Jonson roles is beginning to take shape, and the notion that he had enough skill to take on Kyd's Hieronimo may no longer look so far-fetched.

Other details of Dekker's/Tucca's mockery match what we know of Pembroke's Men with some precision. A particularly telling example is the charge that Jonson/Horace acted in borrowed outfits, a jibe *Satiromastix* repeats with variations. This provides a direct connection to the most frequently cited reference to the company, in a letter Henslowe wrote to Edward Alleyn in September 1593, while London's theatres were in the middle of a devastatingly long closure. This letter has routinely been read as announcing the collapse of Pembroke's company, but what Henslowe in fact writes is that they had been idling in London for the past five or six weeks, too cash-strapped to continue touring, and were "fayne to pane the<r> parell for ther carge" (HD 280) – that is, they were forced to consider pawning their stock of costumes to sustain themselves. Given that they may have had to pawn or even sell part of their "parell," their stock of costumes was likely depleted for years. There is evidence that they had not yet rebuilt it by the time they signed the agreement with Langley in February 1597. As the five defendants concede in one of their depositions, the contract included Langley's offer to provide "apparel fit and necessary for their playing," but they add that they paid him more than £100 for those costumes, and he should now hand them over to the players. Instead, Langley "took the said apparel and converted the same to his best profit by lending the same for hire, whereby he hath received great gains" (EPT 445). Spending in excess of £100 on new apparel over five months would have been an exceptional expense, more than the Admiral's Men spent over a comparable period in any of the years recorded by Henslowe.[150] As soon as the closure of London's theatres put a strain on their finances, the players

---

[150] See Carson, *Companion*, 51.

responded, as they had in 1593, by temporarily liquidating their stock: in early November 1597, Henslowe lent Thomas Downton £12 10s. to "feache ij clockes owt of pane" – garments Downton must have pawned as a member of Pembroke's Men, before returning to the Admiral's Men (HD 99). Even after joining the company at the Rose, the former Pembroke's players continued to negotiate with Langley over costumes. In October 1598, they paid £19 to Langley to recover "a Riche clocke" from him (HD 99). All of this adds up to a picture of a company which, despite the prominence and seniority of its members, had for years struggled to maintain a respectable collection of stage garments. In this context, that Jonson should have been forced to wear another actor's hand-me-downs and even borrow the kind of gown befitting the Knight Marshal of Spain from a player in another company sounds less like a statement about his own marginal status than like a reflection on the realities of Pembroke's Men's specific situation.[151]

The pertinent question at this point may not be "is it plausible that a mere hired hand would have played Hieronimo?" but rather "did Pembroke's Men own *The Spanish Tragedy*?" Interestingly, scholars commenting on *Satiromastix* or drawing on the play for biographical information have sometimes made similar assumptions to the attributionists whose arguments I discussed in Section 3: that Kyd's play, by the mid-1590s, was a kind of free-for-all and had a home in many a repertory. As careful a scholar as Ian Donaldson, for instance, thought it "would have been an obvious piece for a touring company to have taken to the provinces in the 1590s."[152] Whether any company would have staged a play they were not licensed to perform and which belonged to a rival troupe, even in the provinces, is an open question, but it certainly seems unlikely that a frequently London-based company such as Pembroke's Men would have done so. They, after all, had an established repertory of plays. Adding as well known a text as

---

[151] Marcus's reading of *A Shrew* as a play informed by the experience of a struggling acting company fits the same narrative: it is a perspective with which Pembroke's Men would have been all too familiar by 1594 (see *Unediting*, 112–14).

[152] Donaldson, *Jonson*, 106.

The Spanish Tragedy to their roster simply for touring would have been an inconvenience rather than a benefit. To argue that the Hieronimo Jonson played on tour was Kyd's, then, means arguing that *The Spanish Tragedy* was part of the Pembroke regular repertory (and *only* their repertory) in or around 1595/6, and presumably remained there until the "Isle of Dogs" disaster.

In principle, I find this a hypothesis worth examining. I have argued elsewhere that certain plays migrated from companies performing at the Rose to Pembroke's Men and from there on to the Chamberlain's Men; as mentioned in Section 1, I have previously made the case that *Titus Andronicus* belonged to Pembroke's Men until at least the end of 1596, and probably until the "Isle of Dogs" incident.[153] It may be that *The Spanish Tragedy* took a similarly circuitous route from the Rose to the Theatre. However, no other such migrations of plays from Strange's Men can be identified in Henslowe's "Diary" or elsewhere. A few titles in their repertory remained at the Rose, as we saw, most notably Marlowe's *The Jew of Malta* and, as Alleyn's property, *The Massacre at Paris*. Setting "Jeronymo" aside, however, none of the other scripts Strange's Men performed at the Rose can be traced anywhere except to the Chamberlain's Men's repertory. Since no known former member of Lord Strange's troupe joined Pembroke's Men, it is unclear how *The Spanish Tragedy* would have found its way there, and it is in any case difficult to see why the bulk of Strange's Men sharers that went on to form the Chamberlain's Men would have given up a play that they relied on so much at the Rose.

On balance, I consider a different, and by now familiar, proposition more persuasive: that the repertory of Pembroke's Men, like that of the Admiral's Men, contained their own treatment of the Hieronimo story, one which also featured Horatio's death and Hieronimo's madness, but which may have departed in plot and design significantly from Kyd's tragedy. In this scenario, we could imagine Jonson as a Hieronimo who ran mad impressively but didn't occupy as large a share of the text, a memorable role that evidently stuck with Jonson for decades, but not perhaps a star turn. Even if, as I have argued here, Jonson was a sharer and an active,

<hr>

[153] Syme, "Three's Company," 275–84.

competent actor in Pembroke's company, it may be difficult to believe that he was trusted with one of the most prominent roles in the Elizabethan repertory, a part that takes up almost 27 per cent of the text and was among the twenty longest written in the 1580s and 1590s.

Although we may not know *which* Hieronimo Jonson played, there is no real reason, then, to doubt Dekker's word that he played *some version* of the character. What follows from that observation is the necessary, if striking, conclusion that the actor Ben Jonson, like Burbage, can be more securely linked to performances of Hieronimo than Edward Alleyn. We may also recognize that Jonson's nearly lifelong obsession with not just Kyd's play, but audiences' attitudes to new and old versions of the Hieronimo plot, was grounded in his firsthand theatrical experience with the role. We might even consider his full-scale rewriting of a Hieronimo play for the Admiral's Men as an effort to replace his past, actorly connection to the part with an appropriately writerly one. Reading Jonson's theatrical and dramatic career through *Satiromastix* and the Hieronimo complex, then, means allowing Jonson to stand as an artist who bridges the apparent divide between text and stage, a former actor who, even on the page, never left the theatre behind.[154]

5 *The Spanish Tragedy* Rehomed

If the Hieronimo play Jonson performed with Pembroke's Men was not *The Spanish Tragedy*, Kyd's script presumably became part of the starting repertory of the newly founded Chamberlain's Men in 1594. We do not know where the play was before its first appearance in Henslowe's "Diary" in 1592. Manley and MacLean have argued that it may have been composed in 1589, late enough that it could have been written for Strange's Men, who had established themselves in London by November of that year (LSM 80). Alternatively, it may have belonged to another company a year or two earlier and come to Strange's players along with a former member of that

---

[154] For a rich exploration of Jonson as a maker of theatrical books, see Claire M. L. Bourne, *Typographies of Performance in Early Modern England* (Oxford University Press, 2020), 88–105.

unidentifiable troupe. Either way, there is good reason to think that the play was in their repertory by the time Alleyn joined them in the second half of 1591, and that the role of Hieronimo was already taken. When *The Spanish Tragedy* then went to Shoreditch with the former servants of Lord Strange who formed the nucleus of the Chamberlain's Men – George Bryan, John Heminges, Will Kemp, Thomas Pope, and, possibly not until a few years later, Augustine Phillips – one of these highly experienced, well-known actors may still have been playing Hieronimo. Richard Burbage, a new sharer in the company without much of an established track record, probably did not immediately take over the part. His eventual move into the role, however, might have furnished the occasion for commissioning the additions.

Other plays shared *The Spanish Tragedy*'s hypothetical trajectory. Take "Harey the vj," Strange's Men's extraordinarily successful chronicle history play: many scholars are persuaded that this was the play Thomas Nashe describes in his *Pierce Penniless*, a few pages before launching into an ode to "Ned Alleyn." There is now broad agreement that "Harey the vj" ended up with the Chamberlain's Men, where, as the New Oxford Shakespeare editors have recently argued, it was adapted by Shakespeare into the *1 Henry VI* printed in 1623.[155] The "Bacon" play discussed in Section 2 is another script we can situate in Strange's Men's repertory and which bears traces of revision for the Chamberlain's company, and there is the "comodey of Jeronymo."

This companion piece to *The Spanish Tragedy* was more likely a prequel than the first part of a two-play sequence; the two titles were performed consecutively on four occasions by Strange's Men, but Kyd's tragedy appeared more frequently on its own than paired with the "comodey." All the same, the two plays clearly belonged together in some sense, and it is reasonable to assume that the Chamberlain's Men kept both. This scenario finds support in the argument that the "Spanish Comedy" can be linked to

---

[155] See Thomas Nashe, "Pierce Penilesse His Supplication to the Divell," in *The Works of Thomas Nashe*, ed. Ronald B. McKerrow and F. P. Wilson, vol. 1 (Blackwell, 1958), 212–15; LSM 96–9; Taylor and Loughnane, "Canon and Chronology," 513–17.

the anonymous *The First Part of Jeronimo*, published without company attribution in 1605. This version of the text seems to have been staged by a children's company, as it includes numerous mocking references to Hieronimo's diminutive stature. Consequently, it has often been identified as the referent of Webster's "Jeronimo in decimo-sexto" in the Induction to *The Malcontent* – which would confirm the connection between the "Spanish Comedy" and the Chamberlain's/King's Men's repertory. That the 1605 text and the "Spanish Comedy" are closely related has been persuasively argued by Erne. Stylistically and in their content, many passages in *The First Part of Jeronimo* are consistent with a hypothetical prequel to Kyd's play written in the late 1580s; other sequences diverge in style from those passages and match up poorly with the plot of *The Spanish Tragedy*, but they allow the play to stand on its own and can be understood as satirizing Kyd's tragedy. The play printed in 1605, in Erne's interpretation, is more than simply the stolen "comodey of Jeronymo" in a text corrupted by the Children of the Chapel, but an amalgamation of sections of the "Spanish Comedy" with a parody of the *Spanish Tragedy*.[156] When the King's Men in turn adapted and staged *The Malcontent*, they were thus responding in kind to the Children's purloining and lampooning of a mainstay of their repertory.

The Spanish Tragedy *in Shoreditch: Enter Shakespeare, Enter Burbage*

How firmly Kyd's play was established in the repertory of the Chamberlain's Men is traceable in the extraordinarily rich archive of allusions to Hieronimo. No other company's repertory contained more plays with specific allusions to *The Spanish Tragedy* than that of the Chamberlain's and King's Men. Of the thirty-eight plays that refer to it, they owned Jonson's *Every Man in His Humour* (1598), *The Alchemist* (1610), and *The New Inn* (1629), Dekker's *Satiromastix* (1601), Fletcher's *The Tamer Tamed* (1611), *The Captain* (1612–13), and *The Chances* (1617), and Shakespeare's *Taming of the Shrew* (sometime before 1613). Meanwhile, the Admiral's Men and their successor companies staged only two

---

[156] See Erne, *Beyond*, 14–46. Manley and MacLean have recently accepted and extended Erne's arguments (LSM 81–5).

texts with (brief) allusions to *The Spanish Tragedy*, neither listed in Smith's survey (see fn130): Dekker's *The Shoemaker's Holiday* (1599), which uses Kyd's most frequently quoted line, "Go bye, Jeronimo," and Middleton and Rowley's *The Roaring Girl* (1611), which recycles a Spanish tag familiar from Kyd, "pocas palabras."[157]

The other notable aspect of the long catalogue of allusions is that all but one of them date from 1598 or after, with a cluster of references occurring from 1598 to 1605. As I argued in Section 3, this was the very moment when "Jeronimo" could no longer stand straightforwardly for the text written in the late 1580s and first printed in 1592. Strikingly, several early references highlight that there is something new about Hieronimo and about *The Spanish Tragedy* itself. The nostalgic audience member lampooned in *Cynthia's Revels* is the clearest instance, but in a slightly more oblique vein, Marston's parody in *Antonio and Mellida*, by taking aim at Shakespeare's recent addition, also focusses on innovation. The play as represented in the market for printed books changed in those years, too, with the 1602 quarto's title page announcing a text "enlarged with new additions of the Painters part, and others."[158]

The Spanish Tragedy would not gain its quirky subtitle of "Hieronimo is mad *again*" until the 1615 quarto, but the sense of repetition with a difference is already palpable in the late Elizabethan allusions. Something gave the play and its performance new purchase and visibility then. It will not be surprising at this point for me to argue that "Shakespeare" was behind that difference. I do not think that the additions are the only answer, though. Rather, I would propose that the sense of newness and the play's renewed impact in performance had as much to do with Burbage as with the added text.[159] We should also not

---

[157] Dekker had a veritable *Spanish Tragedy* fixation, quoting from the play on eight different occasions; the reference in *The Shoemaker's Holiday* may have more to do with this preoccupation than with his writing the play for the Admiral's Men. See also Frank Ardolino, "Thomas Dekker's Use of Kyd's *The Spanish Tragedy* in *Satiromastix*," *English Language Notes* 41 (2003): 7–18.

[158] ESTC S109291.

[159] Douglas Bruster likewise suggests that the additions were written specifically for Burbage, though without making a theatre-historical case for his theory. See "Shakespeare's hand in the additional passages to Kyd's *Spanish Tragedy*," OUP

overlook another change that took place around the same time: by 1598, the Chamberlain's Men had lost their old home at the Theatre and had moved to the neighbouring venue, the much larger and non-polygonal Curtain playhouse.[160]

If Hieronimo became a Burbage role around 1598, the casting switch provides a rationale for the additions. The play changed because the player who acted the lead changed.[161] Identifying who might have played Hieronimo until then requires speculation, but we can at least narrow down our list of candidates. Among the senior actors verifiable as founding members of the Chamberlain's Men, Thomas Pope is an unlikely choice as he was mainly known for his comedic talent; Will Kemp, as the company's principal clown, is similarly improbable. That leaves George Bryan and John Heminges. Heminges is frequently called "old" by the 1610s, which might have made him a suitable Hieronimo even years earlier.[162] However, it is not obvious why he would have given up the part by 1598, when he was still far from retirement. In Bryan's case, a possible explanation offers itself. He remained an active sharer until 1597/8, when he is listed in the "Seven Deadly Sins" plot as playing a counselor to Burbage's King Gorboduc. This does not look like a large role, but the character's social status corresponds to Hieronimo's. However, by late 1598, when Richard and Cuthbert Burbage assembled a consortium of sharers to cofinance the building of the Globe, Bryan was the *only* former Strange's player absent from the group. He is also not listed among the "principal comedians" Jonson names in his 1616 *Workes* as the September 1598 cast of *Every Man in His Humour* – again the

Blog, 23 August 2013 (https://blog.oup.com/2013/08/shakespeares-additional-passage-kyd-spanish-tragedy).

[160] McInnis offers perceptive commentary on the opportunities the new space might have offered (*Shakespeare and Lost Plays*, 70–87).

[161] The economic arguments against revisions I endorsed in Section 1 do not quite apply to the Chamberlain's/King's Men during Shakespeare's career since his responsibilities as a company member probably included writing new plays and revamping old ones without additional compensation; this would explain why so many of Shakespeare's plays were revised.

[162] See Nungezer, *Dictionary*, 181–2.

only Strange's Men veteran missing. That Bryan retired from acting and became a Groom of the Chamber by 1601 has long been known, but I think we can now hypothesize that his departure took place sometime in 1598.[163] That Bryan would have played a role of the caliber of Hieronimo is entirely plausible: sharers in early modern acting companies were equal "fellows," and, as I have argued elsewhere, it is a misconception to think that one or two actors regularly performed all major leads (see fn21). Bryan was an extremely experienced player whose subsequent appointment to the royal court implies that he was in official favour. He is about as good a fit as any member of Strange's Men for the lead in *The Spanish Tragedy*, even if Burbage's fame in the role soon eclipsed whatever institutional memory may have existed of George Bryan's performance.

The sense of an old and familiar play – even an old and familiar performance, since presumably many other parts, at least the male characters, continued to be played by the same actors as before – having become new again is captured, somewhat obliquely and with Jonsonian irony, in the very first explicit reference to *The Spanish Tragedy* anywhere in early modern drama, in *Every Man in His Humour*. There, the braggart soldier Bobadilla and the foolish would-be poet Matheo cannot praise the play enough. The latter waxes ecstatic over the infamous "O eyes, no eyes, but fountains fraught with tears" (3.2.1–11) passage, while Bobadilla declares that "all the poets of our time" have failed to "pen such another play as that was."[164] Jonson may be biting the hand that feeds him, a lifelong habit, poking fun at the dated style of a play in the same repertory for which his comedy was written. The joke is also a more complex riff on audiences so obsessed with objects of nostalgia that they cannot even recognize that it is the very "poets of our time" who inject new lifeblood into old offerings such as *The Spanish Tragedy* – precisely the exercise in rejuvenation that the Chamberlain's Men and Shakespeare were in the process of undertaking with Kyd's play when *Every Man In* appeared on their stage. Since the two plays almost certainly

---

[163] See Mark Eccles, "Elizabethan Actors I: A–D," *Notes and Queries* 38 (1991): 38–49, 42.

[164] Ben Jonson, *Every Man in His Humour (Quarto Version)*, ed. David Bevington (CWBJ), 1.3.101–13.

were in active repertory at the same time, the actors performing Bobadilla and Matheo would also speak some of Kyd's matchless lines in *The Spanish Tragedy*. Sadly, we cannot know if Burbage played either character.

As we can see in Edward Guilpin's *Skialethia*, entered in the Stationers' Register in September 1598, the newly noteworthy *Spanish Tragedy* was associated specifically with the Curtain. In *Skialethia*, a satirist conjures up a virtual London in his study, where he can go to the playhouse (or the law courts in Westminster Hall) simply by picking up a book:

> Heere may I sit, yet walke to *Westminster*
> And heare *Fitzherbert*, *Plowden*, *Brooke*, and *Dier*
> Canuas a law-case: or if my dispose
> Perswade me to a play, I'le to the *Rose*,
> Or *Curtaine*, one of *Plautus* Comedies,
> Or the *Patheticke Spaniard* Tragedies.

Guilpin is extremely up to date in this poem: he also compares a melancholic figure to the abandoned Theatre, recently vacated by the Chamberlain's Men when Cuthbert Burbage's extended negotiations for a new lease had finally broken down:

> But see yonder,
> One like the vnfrequented Theater
> Walkes in darke silence, and vast solitude,
> Suited to those blacke fancies which intrude,
> Vpon possession of his troubled breast.[165]

For Guilpin, the Curtain and the Rose were linked to specific kinds of plays, all, as the logic of the satire implies, available in print: at the Rose, he expects comedies – something modelled on Plautus, apparently, though what that might be is unclear; at the Curtain, Spanish Tragedies. The Chamberlain's Men not only played "the *Patheticke Spaniards* Tragedies"

---

[165] Edward Guilpin, *Skialetheia. Or, A Shadowe of Truth* (London: I[ames] R[oberts] for Nicholas Ling, 1598), sig. D4v.

there, but also *Romeo and Juliet*: as we know from Marston's *Scourge of Villany*, Shakespeare's tragedy was receiving "Curtain plaudities" that year, but that is presumably not what Guilpin meant.[166] His plural, though, is interesting: perhaps it suggests that both the Chamberlain's Men's Hieronimo plays remained in their active repertory. Or perhaps it should encourage us to read Guilpin's syntax differently, as implying that Plautus-inspired comedies and tragedies about pathetic Spaniards were on offer at both the Rose and the Curtain, which, by 1598, was also true.

Pace Andrew Gurr, *The Spanish Tragedy* was not "an emblem" of any one Elizabethan playhouse: the companies that owned it shifted performance venues too often in the 1590s. After the initial year on record at the Rose, the play spent a few years at the Theatre and barely a year at the Curtain before arriving at the Globe and subsequently expanding to the Blackfriars. All the same, it became part of the fabric of the place and of the company that inhabited it. By 1614, when Jonson returned to his familiar theme of audiences obsessed with long-established staples in *Bartholomew Fair*, the distinction between old and new Hieronimo had collapsed: *The Spanish Tragedy* had become a classic, the evolution it underwent around 1598 now invisible. Jonson, writing for the recently rebuilt Globe's neighbourhood rival, the Hope, lumps it together with another King's Men classic when he offers sarcastic praise for spectators whose "judgement shows it is constant, and hath stood still, these five and twenty, or thirty years" – spectators who still "will swear *Jeronimo* or *Andronicus* are the best plays yet."[167]

The Spanish Tragedy *as a Chamberlain's/King's Men Play: New Readings*

I want to conclude this section with a brief discussion of two other Jonsonian engagements with *The Spanish Tragedy* to show how their

---

[166] Quoted in EPT 412. Marston's volume was entered into the Stationer's Register on 8 September 1598, seven days before Guilpin's book (EPT 411).

[167] *Bartholomew Fair*, ed. John Creaser (CWBJ), Induction 105–10. Gurr seems to have this passage in mind when he writes of "Jonson's derision which characterised [*The Spanish Tragedy*] as a typical Fortune play" (*Shakespeare's*

significance changes now that we can understand them in the context of the Chamberlain's/King's Men's repertory.

The first example, *Poetaster* (1601), was not written for the Chamberlain's Men, but rather in anticipation of a play they were about to stage, Dekker's *Satiromastix*. Nevertheless, or for that very reason, it contains Jonson's most extended quotations from *The Spanish Tragedy*, in a scene in which the irascible Captain Tucca has his pages (the Pyrgi) put on a medley of dramatic excerpts for Histrio, the player. In all, the performance quotes passages from eleven plays. What has long been something of a puzzle is why so many of them seem to come from the repertory of the Admiral's Men, even though that company was not, as far as we know, involved in the back-and-forth squabble among playwrights some scholars still refer to as the "poets' war." The extant plays in which Marston, Dekker, Jonson, and possibly Shakespeare traded insults and mockery were staged by the Children of the Chapel, the Children of Paul's, and the Chamberlain's Men. *Poetaster* explicitly presages a performance of *Satiromastix* at the Globe. Why, then, would Jonson focus his satire primarily on the Admiral's Men's plays?

As we can now appreciate, he did not. The *Cambridge Ben Jonson* has newly designated three of the quotations as references to Shakespeare – all of them lines spoken by Pistol (*2 Henry IV*, 2.4.136–8 and 5.3.99; *Merry Wives of Windsor*, 1.3.30) and themselves parodies of bombastic dramatic speech.[168] One passage is taken from *The Battle of Alcazar*, certainly an Admiral's Men's play and probably on stage as a revival around the same time as *Poetaster*. Three speeches are from unidentified plays. One is a medley of motifs reminiscent of moments in *Doctor Faustus* (Admiral's Men), *Antonio's Revenge* (Boys of Paul's), *A Warning for Fair Women* (Chamberlain's Men), and perhaps *Hamlet* (Chamberlain's Men). One is a quotation from the Admiral's Men's *Blind Beggar of Alexandria* that itself

---

Opposites, 189), but nothing in *Bartholomew Fair* suggests a reference to that playhouse.

[168] *Poetaster*, ed. Gabriele Bernhard Jackson (CWBJ), 3.4.212–14 and commentary. All references to Shakespeare's works are to the *Norton Shakespeare*, 3rd ed., ed. Stephen Greenblatt et al. (Norton, 2015).

obliquely parodies a line in *The Spanish Tragedy*. And the two longest passages come from *The Spanish Tragedy* – quotations that we can now recognize as references to the Chamberlain's Men's repertory (see 3.4.169–286 and commentary). At least seven of the eleven speeches (indirectly, eight) point to the Globe company, while just two or three touch on the repertory of the Admiral's Men.

The sense that the scene with Tucca's pages takes aim at the adult companies in general but has a special relationship with the Chamberlain's Men is enhanced if we follow James Bednarz's reading of Histrio as a representative of the Globe company. Bednarz tentatively identifies him with Augustine Phillips, the sharer who seems to have acted in a quasi-managerial position for the Chamberlain's Men by 1601.[169] From that perspective, the scene resembles that between Burbage, Kemp, and the student in *2 Return from Parnassus*: a group of amateurs auditioning for a professional actor by performing speeches from his company's own repertory. If we take the scene somewhat seriously as a humorous portrayal of an audition, a potential distinction emerges between Jonson's treatment of plays from the Chamberlain's Men's repertory and his use of the Admiral's Men's stock.[170]

The more the pages perform from *The Spanish Tragedy* or Pistol's parodic lines, the more impressed Histrio is, eventually asking Tucca's price to let them act with his company. How overtly Kyd's play is being satirized is not entirely obvious, and when the pages riff on Pistol's lines the playfulness of their acting could be seen as *serving* the parodic quality of the text they perform. That text notably pokes fun at the rhetoric of older titles

---

[169] James Bednarz, *Shakespeare and the Poets' War* (Columbia University Press, 2001), 233–7.

[170] Recognizing that *The Spanish Tragedy* was not an Admiral's Men's play makes the scene newly coherent. Conversely, Jackson reads the Pyrgi's performance as primarily a tissue of allusions to the Admiral's repertory (3.4.184 commentary); she therefore has to posit that Histrio's identity fluctuates. He suddenly "has turned into a Globe actor" when he tells Tucca that his company has hired Demetrius (Jonson's stand-in for Dekker) "to abuse Horace [i.e., Jonson] and bring him in in a play" (3.4.262 and commentary). In the reading I propose here, Histrio is consistently portrayed as a "Globe player."

in the Admiral's Men's repertory, and this overt targeting of the Fortune company comes to a head in the Pyrgi's most elaborate send-up, staged after the audition is over and Histrio is about to leave. At that point, they play a passage from *The Battle of Alcazar* as an unmistakable parody of not just the play's style, but the most celebrated Admiral's Man, Alleyn himself. "The boy comes in on Minos's shoulders, who stalks as he acts," Jonson's stage direction reads (3.4.278SD). It takes two boy actors to produce a figure of sufficient height to mimic Alleyn's exceptionally tall stature; his stalking too was notorious.[171] The text the page speaks is not itself satirical: it is a serious passage being made fun of, just as Alleyn's habits as a performer are specifically lampooned by the boy actors. If we think back to Section 1, the cutting topicality of the parody should be apparent: after all, Alleyn had just returned to the stage after a three-year hiatus, and one of the plays the Admiral's Men had revived to mark the occasion was *The Battle of Alcazar*.

Knutson is right to stress that we should not "underestimat[e] the commercial value of the advertising" that Jonson's satirical "choice of play-scraps" performs for the adult companies.[172] I am not sure this is equally true for all the plays and companies being mocked, though. *Poetaster* makes fun of the Boys of Paul's and the Chamberlain's Men, but it also acknowledges that they are in on the game and that the satirizing of dramatic rhetoric is a shared interest – in the same way that the "poets' war" itself was both an antagonistic and a collaborative effort. Just as the Admiral's Men seem to have remained on the outside of that effort, however, they come in for a different kind of treatment in *Poetaster*'s game, where they are more explicitly and uncharitably burlesqued than their colleagues at the Globe. Identifying *The Spanish Tragedy* as part of the Chamberlain's Men's repertory allows us to perceive that distinction: it makes it possible to read the references to Kyd's play as relatively gentle mockery when compared to the multilevel ridiculing of *The Battle of Alcazar* and its performance.

---

[171] See Andrew Gurr, "Who Strutted and Bellowed?" *Shakespeare Survey* 16 (1963): 95–102. Incidentally, in this early essay, Gurr never connects Alleyn to Hieronimo, describing the role instead as "one of Burbage's most famous parts" (97).

[172] Knutson, *Playing Companies*, 131.

In my second example, from *The Alchemist* (1610), the trick Jonson was playing can only be understood now that we grasp that *The Spanish Tragedy* and Burbage had an extended shared history in the repertory of the King's Men. In a sense, it is the long-delayed payoff to the inter-repertorial joke *Every Man in His Humour* set up twelve years before. In *The Alchemist*, Jonson relies on his audience's familiarity with not only *The Spanish Tragedy*, but the props, costumes, and established cast from the King's Men's performances of it. He is explicit and specific in his repertorial cross-references: Abel Drugger is supposed to borrow "Hieronimo's old cloak, ruff, and hat" from "the players,"[173] thus setting up an expectation for metatheatrical play that is fulfilled when Subtle later enters to hand Face "your Hieronimo's cloak, and hat," "and the ruff too" (5.4.68–9).[174] Given the play's obsession with parallels between its plot of deceptions and the deception of the theatre, with the Blackfriars as a place to see plays and a place (in the play) where cheating happens, the arrival of Hieronimo's *actual* costume brings unique focus to metatheatrical self-reflection. The costume remains necessarily outside of the fictional world of the play, recognizable, *as Hieronimo's*, as an item that belongs to a different performance, if one that on another day could be seen on the same stage, with the same actors; and yet it is integrated, without losing that alien identity, into the fiction of *The Alchemist*.[175] At the same time, the moment toys with the audience's expectations of who will get to wear that outfit, of just how far Jonson is going to push the joke. In the end, it is Lovewit rather than Drugger who puts on the cloak. Its first, long-delayed appearance on stage, in Subtle's hands, hints at a different possibility. That Jonson has *Subtle*

---

[173] *The Alchemist*, ed. Peter Holland and William Sherman (CWBJ), 4.7.71, 68.

[174] We might note that Hieronimo's cloak always seems to be older as a costume than a Knight Marshall of Spain's cloak has any business being in the world of the play: always cast off, borrowed, secondhand. Is Jonson still justifying his own costume from fourteen or fifteen years before?

[175] The point is precisely *not*, as the CWBJ editors think, that "the play was long out-of-date" (4.7.71 commentary), but that it, and its costumes and props, were instantly recognizable to audiences at both Blackfriars and Globe. It is a joke that depends on currency.

bring in the costume is as dramaturgically arbitrary as it is theatrically deliberate. It meant that the actor bringing on Hieronimo's old and familiar outfit was the actor as intimately associated with those clothes as with Hamlet's inky cloak, Othello's handkerchief, or Lear's too-tightly-buttoned doublet. He brought on his own costume: Subtle was played by Richard Burbage.[176]

Epilogue: Productive Error

What happened to the various Hieronimo plays after 1620 is unclear. As we saw in Section 2, the Palsgrave's Men did not survive the lengthy closure of theatres after James I's death. The King's Men fared much better, but *The Spanish Tragedy* may eventually have dropped out of their repertory. One of the last dramatic references to Kyd's play occurs in Thomas Rawlins's *The Rebellion*, a tragedy entered into the Stationers' Register in 1639 and probably performed in 1636 by the King's Revels Company (BDC #2413). An extended comic scene, rich in verbatim quotations from *The Spanish Tragedy*, features a tailor who, Bottom-like, wants to act the parts in a proposed amateur performance of "Jeronimo." He boasts that he will "gape wider than the widest / Mouth'd Fowler of them all" when playing Hieronimo.[177] The wide-mouthed Fowler must be Richard Fowler, a player who by 1636 was a sharer in the infant Prince Charles's company, performing at the Red Bull.[178] If we take Rawlins literally, Kyd's play had made it to yet another playhouse, where, abandoned by its former owners, it was once more being given new, if old-fashioned, life. On the other hand, Prince Charles's Men would certainly have needed a license for an old play newly added to their repertory, and no such record survives. It is perhaps just as likely that Rawlins's tailor does not have an actual performance by Fowler as Hieronimo in mind, but rather imagines his own take on the role to be

---

[176] See James A. Riddell, "Some Actors in Ben Jonson's Plays," *Shakespeare Studies* 5 (1969): 285–98.

[177] Quoted in Smith, "Hieronimo's Afterlives," 137–8.

[178] See Gerald Eades Bentley, *The Jacobean and Caroline Stage*, (Clarendon, 1941), 7 vols., 1:302–15.

vocally as powerful as Fowler's would be – if Fowler had ever got to play the part.

By the time Kirkman assembled his catalogue in 1661, the title of *The Spanish Tragedy* as well as Kyd's authorship had faded from view. Both remained absent in three Restoration accounts of English literary history.[179] By 1691, Gerard Langbaine would classify Kyd as merely "an Ancient Writer, or rather Translator in the time of Queen *Elizabeth*," while confidently claiming that "*Hieronymo* [is] an Anonymous play."[180] The reduction of the former cluster to single play was complete. Yet Langbaine might point us, unexpectedly, to more information about the Admiral's Men's "Joronymo." He declared "*Hieronymo*" anonymous in an entry on William Smith, correcting two earlier chroniclers of English literature, Edward Phillips and William Winstanley. Both had described Smith as "the Author of a Tragedy entituled *Hieronymo*; as also *The Hector of Germany*."[181] Langbaine considers this ascription a result of "their old Mistake": Smith did in fact write *The Hector of Germany*, as well as a play celebrating the Worthy Company of Tailors, and coauthored an antiquarian volume on the County Palatine of Chester. But, Langbaine insists, he had nothing to do with Hieronimo.[182]

Phillips's assertion (which Winstanley copied verbatim) certainly seems to have come out of nowhere: no one else had associated William Smith with a Hieronimo tragedy, and from the perspective of modern scholarship, the idea that Smith wrote a popular stage play is irreconcilable with what we now know about him. In the late 1580s, he was living in Chester, writing

[179] See Emma Smith, "Author v. Character in Early Modern Dramatic Authorship: The Example of Thomas Kyd and *The Spanish Tragedy*," *Medieval and Renaissance Drama in England* 11 (1999): 129–42, 131–2.

[180] Gerard Langbaine, *An Account of the English Dramatick Poets* (Oxford: L. L. for George West and Henry Clements, 1691), sig. Hh4v–Hh5r.

[181] Phillips, *Theatrum Poetarum* (London: Printed for Charles Smith, 1675), sig. Ii2r; Winstanley, *The Lives of the Most Famous English Poets* (London: H. Clark for Samuel Manship, 1687), sig. P5v.

[182] Nevertheless, William Smith remained more visible than Kyd as *The Spanish Tragedy*'s possible author into the mid-eighteenth century; see Jeremy Lopez, *Constructing the Canon of Early Modern Drama* (Cambridge University Press, 2014), 27–8.

works of antiquarian interest; by the mid 1590s, he was "campaigning for a position in the College of Arms," a goal he attained in 1597. While he almost certainly *did* write *The Hector of Germany*, that play was an occasional piece to celebrate the marriage of Princess Elizabeth to the Elector Palatine in 1613, performed "by a Company of Young-men of this Citie."[183] Smith's biography makes it as unlikely that he had anything to do with the original *Spanish Tragedy* as that he wrote "Joronymo" in 1597.

What if Phillips's "old Mistake" was akin to an error more recent scholars have also made: confusing two W. Smiths? As David Kathman notes, "since the late nineteenth century," *The Hector of Germany* had mistakenly "been attributed to the Elizabethan playwright Wentworth Smith."[184] That dramatist was unknown to Phillips, Winstanley, and Langbaine, mostly because none of his plays were ever printed. He is a regular, though, in Henslowe's "Diary," where payments for fifteen plays he either wrote or cowrote are recorded between April 1601 and March 1603. Smith was born in 1571 and was working as a scrivener in London by 1596, a background he shared with Kyd.[185] He was certainly old enough to write a play for the Admiral's Men in 1597. That his name does not appear in Henslowe's records for the first three years in which they contain payments to playwrights may not be significant. Some writers, including Jonson, disappear from the "Diary" for years at a time. The specifics of what we know about "Joronymo" might even explain Smith's absence: after all, the novice playwright who managed to turn a new Hieronimo play into a commercial mediocrity was perhaps not a prime candidate for immediate rehire.

"Wentworth Smith the Author of a Tragedy entituled *Hieronymo*" is little more than reckless speculation, but it is a possible answer to two puzzles: Who wrote a play about Hieronimo for the Admiral's Men in 1597? And why did Edward Phillips think that a man called Smith was the author of a "Tragedy entituled *Hieronymo*"? It also provides a pleasing and aptly

---

[183] David Kathman, "Smith, William (c. 1550–1618)," *Oxford Dictionary of National Biography Online*, www.oxforddnb.com/view/article/25922.

[184] Ibid.

[185] David Kathman, "Smith, Wentworth (Bap. 1571)," *Oxford Dictionary of National Biography Online*, www.oxforddnb.com/view/article/25919.

ironic coda to the history I have traced here. These Restoration literary historians failed to identify *The Spanish Tragedy* as the play that launched the Hieronimo complex. However, they unexpectedly and unknowingly may have cast light on the moment when Kyd's work, in being eclipsed, reached the peak of its influence: the late 1590s, when "Jeronimo," no longer merely a play, became a cultural phenomenon.

Starting from a minor question of attribution (who wrote the 2,672 words newly printed in 1602?), I have ended on an even more ephemeral and certainly far more speculative attribution argument: that a lost play may have been written by a forgotten playwright whose other works have also all disappeared. The questions with which I have grappled along the way, though, could hardly be of more consequence for an understanding of early modern drama: How did acting companies structure their repertories? How were new plays written? What was the relationship between existing and new playscripts? How can we understand the commercial dealings between playhouse owners and companies, and how do we read the surviving records of those transactions? As large as these questions may be, answers to them lie only in fragments and minutiae. A minor shift, such as that triggered by the reattribution of the *Spanish Tragedy* additions, can prompt fundamental reconsiderations such as the ones I have offered here. These new hypotheses in turn allow for and necessitate a return to smaller, more specific questions: How do we read one brief moment in *The Alchemist*? And what about Wentworth Smith?

Acknowledgements

As short as it may be, this Element has been a long time in the making. It began life as a blog post and then languished in a virtual drawer as an overlong article before being given a chance to reinvent itself thanks to the vigorous editorial encouragement and interventions of Claire Bourne and Rory Loughnane. Along the way, ideas that had their first airing in talks at Columbia, Harvard, Oxford, and York University found their way into the expanded and refurbished text. I owe an enormous debt to friends and colleagues who engaged with the arguments I am presenting here: Farah Karim-Cooper, Andy Kesson, Pete Kirwan, Jeremy Lopez, James Mardock, David McInnis, Lucy Munro, Richard Preiss, Eoin Price, Emma Smith, Tiffany Stern, Elizabeth Tavares, Misha Teramura, Leslie Thomson, and the much-missed John Astington. Ros Knutson has seen, dissected, helped to reassemble, and prodded along more versions of the text than I dare admit: this Element would not exist without her or her work. I am also grateful to two extraordinarily generous and attentive external reviewers. Alison Syme, as always, read everything from first draft to last.

I dedicate this volume to the memory of my father, Karlheinz Schott, who died as the manuscript went into production. He taught me how to take delight in literature and to love performance; our last conversations were about Thomas Mann and Mozart. I have no idea what I would be doing with my life without his formative influence, but it wouldn't be *this*.

In memory of my father, Karlheinz Schott
13 February 1946–19 December 2022

Cambridge Elements ≡

Shakespeare and Text

Claire M. L. Bourne
The Pennsylvania State University

Claire M. L. Bourne is Assistant Professor of English at the Pennsylvania State University. She is author of *Typographies of Performance in Early Modern England* (2020) and editor of the collection *Shakespeare / Text* (2021). She has published extensively on early modern book design and reading practices in venues such as *PBSA*, *ELR*, *Shakespeare*, and numerous edited collections. She is also co-author (with Jason Scott-Warren) of an article attributing the annotations in the Free Library of Philadelphia's copy of the Shakespeare First Folio to John Milton. She has edited Fletcher and Massinger's *The Sea Voyage* for the *Routledge Anthology of Early Modern Drama* (ed. Jeremy Lopez) and is working on an edition of *Henry the Sixth, Part 1* for the Arden Shakespeare, Fourth Series.

Rory Loughnane
University of Kent

Rory Loughnane is Reader in Early Modern Studies and Co-director of the Centre for Medieval and Early Modern Studies at the University of Kent. He is the author or editor of nine books and has published widely on Shakespeare and textual studies. In his role as Associate Editor of the *New Oxford* Shakespeare, he has edited more than ten of Shakespeare's plays, and co-authored with Gary Taylor a book-length study about the 'Canon and Chronology' of Shakespeare's works. He is a General Editor of the forthcoming

Oxford Marlowe edition, a Series Editor of Studies in Early
Modern Authorship, a General Editor of the CADRE database,
and a General Editor of The Revels Plays series.

ABOUT THE SERIES

Cambridge Elements in Shakespeare and Text offers a platform for
original scholarship about the creation, circulation, reception,
remaking, use, performance, teaching, and translation of the
Shakespearean text across time and place. The series seeks to publish
research that challenges – and pushes beyond – the conventional
parameters of Shakespeare and textual studies.

Cambridge Elements ≡

Shakespeare and Text

Printed in the United States
by Baker & Taylor Publisher Services